PRAISE FOR
EXECUTIVE FUNDAMENTALS

"Let's face it, leading organizations does not come easy for most executives. This book consolidates decades of executive management studies into simple and straightforward fundamentals, a blueprint for successful executive leadership. Focusing on the fundamentals outlined in this book will surely enable sustained success for both aspiring and seasoned executives."

—**Mick Doyle, Vice President, Nordstrom**

"Thought provoking and insightful! This book is a great reminder of the importance of executing the fundamentals. It's not enough to just know what to do . . . you have to be able to do it. This principle is true in sports and in business. I will enthusiastically recommend this book to current and future Leaders."

—**Brent Carr, Senior Vice President, Litehouse Foods**

"Great insights for anyone aspiring to be a leader."

—**Nancy Pollino, Executive Vice President, PNC Bank**

"Leadership skills are the differentiator in building your personal brand. *Executive Fundamentals* provides a practical framework to guide aspiring leaders in their development journey."

—**Mike Koppel, Retired Executive Vice President & CFO, Nordstrom**

"A well laid out framework and ongoing reference for those interested in leadership development."

—**Steve Temares, Chief Executive Officer, Bed Bath & Beyond**

NICHOLAS A. FISCHER
& DANIEL H. SHIN

EXECUTIVE

ESSENTIAL PRINCIPLES
FOR DEVELOPING LEADERS

FUNDAMENTALS

RIVER GROVE
BOOKS

Published by River Grove Books
Austin, TX
www.rivergrovebooks.com

Distributed by River Grove Books

Design and composition by Greenleaf Book Group
Cover design by Greenleaf Book Group

From "Working Together: Principles and Practices"
by Alan Mulally. Copyright © by Alan Mulally. Reproduced by permission of the author.

Publisher's Cataloging-in-Publication data is available.

Print ISBN: 978-1-63299-181-2

eBook ISBN: 978-1-63299-182-9

First Edition

TO OUR WIVES, MEGAN AND YOUNG-IN,
WHO HAVE PROVIDED UNWAVERING
SUPPORT AND ENCOURAGEMENT.

CONTENTS

YOU'VE GOT TO EARN IT

There's only one thing that can compensate for
lack of natural talent, and that's effort.

For most of us, participating in sports is how we learn a foundational and humbling fact: If you want to be good at something, you've got to earn it. Output is a direct function of input. My work ethic was built on the steep inclines of country roads. Every day after school, I would do sprints up a punishing hill to build endurance and speed. I was short and scrawny with limited natural abilities, and I hated losing. The only solution I could come up with was to outwork everyone. It didn't take long for me to discover that only one thing can compensate for lack of natural talent—effort.[1]

Many years later, sports once again led me to new discoveries—ones that triggered the formation of the concepts that are the subject of this book—executive fundamentals. Let me explain.

Dan and I crossed paths in Seattle when we both relocated there for our jobs. Although we had a lot in common, it was our shared interest in golf that ultimately led us to where we are today. Dan was a qualified golfer; I was not. I was new to the sport, and even with a few lessons and a lot of practice at the driving range, my performance and abilities remained limited. I've always been an avid reader, and one day I stumbled upon *Ben Hogan's Five Lessons: The Modern Fundamentals of Golf.* In *Five Lessons*, Hogan breaks golf down into four fundamentals: the grip, the stance and posture, the first part of the swing, and the second part of the swing. Hogan claims in the introduction that anyone (within reason) can shoot under 80 once they've mastered the fundamentals.

> *It's easy knowing what to do. It's much*
> ▸ *more difficult actually doing what you*
> *know you're supposed to do.*

Five Lessons was a quick read, and I finished it in an afternoon. And then I started to believe him. For the first time, I felt that I had the knowledge I had been missing—I understood what I was

---

[1] Throughout this book, personal stories are occasionally shared to illustrate different points; all such stories come from the experiences of Nick Fischer.

supposed to do! I took my newfound confidence to the driving range, where my first swing produced a perfectly sliced shot that wouldn't have hit the fairway two holes over.

That's when I learned an important lesson. It's easy *knowing* what to do. It's much more difficult actually *doing* what you know you're supposed to do. I began to realize that the flawless execution of a perfect swing was only going to come after thousands of repetitions. I needed to commit each and every golf fundamental to muscle memory. I followed Hogan's advice, which emphasized focusing on one fundamental at a time. Living in Seattle was advantageous, since the summer sun would be out before five o'clock a.m. I'd be teeing off as the sun was coming up and would finish nine holes with plenty of time to make it to the office downtown before nine a.m. These early morning rounds were perfect for practicing the fundamentals, because I was always first to tee off, with almost no other golfers around to interfere with my developing game. I progressed consistently, but it was not a linear improvement. Rather, it was a frustrating quest. Some days I felt like everything was finally starting to click, but then I would completely melt down during the following round. It was a lot of hard work, but slowly, eventually, I nudged my game away from its initial embarrassing level.

> *Everything that requires a developed set of skills has a set of fundamentals.*

As you might imagine, discussing what I was learning about my golf fundamentals was a big topic of conversation between Dan and me. It didn't take long before our conversation shifted to what is now an obvious realization: Everything that requires a developed set of skills has a set of fundamentals, and in order for the fundamentals to be accessed readily, many repetitions must be done to create muscle memory.

Since Dan and I are both quite driven to build successful business careers, we asked the following question: What are the fundamental qualities of an exemplary executive? That one question began to take over our golf course conversations and led to countless hours exploring the depths of executive fundamentals. Initially, our determination was driven by our own desires to identify the fundamentals so we could incorporate them into our own development plans.

To our surprise, the early versions of our frameworks became unexpectedly popular with the folks we worked with. As a result, we decided to organize the fundamentals to create this brief and simple guide. We firmly believe that, like any other profession, executive effectiveness is built upon well-developed fundamentals. Thus, this book is designed to provide a general road map that aspiring executives can use to guide their development.

At this point, you may be asking yourself how we define executive effectiveness, because that's the entire purpose of developing executive fundamentals. Our definition is simple: Executive effectiveness is measured by the quality and consistency of the outcomes he or she is responsible for delivering. Because the quality of outcomes is built upon the culmination of every decision made, we believe the purpose of developing executive fundamentals is ultimately to improve decision-making.

We've structured the book in two parts that are aligned with how we think about development: Development is knowing what to do and then doing it. Part I (chapters 1–4) is dedicated to each of the four executive fundamentals, with each fundamental followed by a mini development action plan. Part II (chapters 5–6) is dedicated to executive development and bringing it all together.

PART I — KNOWING WHAT TO DO

In this book, we state that the four fundamentals present in every successful executive are business acumen, management ability, leadership ability, and executive intelligence.

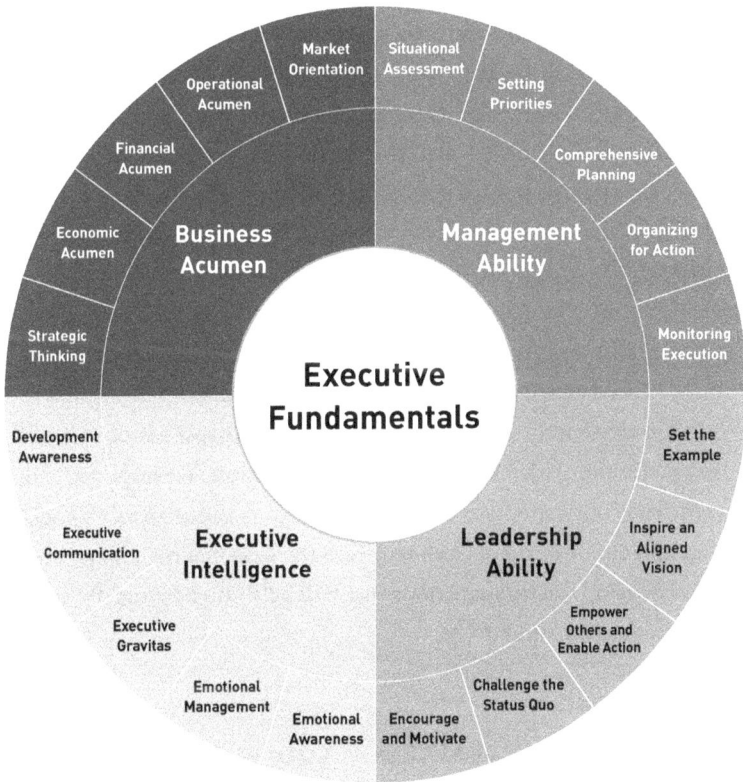

Executive Fundamentals

- Business Acumen
  - Market Orientation
  - Operational Acumen
  - Financial Acumen
  - Economic Acumen
  - Strategic Thinking
- Management Ability
  - Situational Assessment
  - Setting Priorities
  - Comprehensive Planning
  - Organizing for Action
  - Monitoring Execution
- Leadership Ability
  - Set the Example
  - Inspire an Aligned Vision
  - Empower Others and Enable Action
  - Challenge the Status Quo
  - Encourage and Motivate
- Executive Intelligence
  - Development Awareness
  - Executive Communication
  - Executive Gravitas
  - Emotional Management
  - Emotional Awareness

You'll notice that throughout Part I, we make extensive references to other authors and to other works about business that we admire. This is entirely intentional, because the executive fundamentals are built upon a foundation consisting of the collective knowledge we've learned from others. Moreover, we think the sources referenced throughout the book serve as an exceptional reading list for anyone committed to continuous development.

The executive fundamentals presented in our book are based on what we've learned from others and our personal and professional experiences—reading, learning, trying, failing, and adapting. For example, I distinctly remember the first time I presented my leadership philosophy and team vision to my two direct reports. I was a manager, and my entire team consisted of the three of us. It was awkward, and I stumbled through it, but the team appreciated it. Every time I went into a new role or new people joined the team, I took the opportunity to get better and better. By the time I was a director with a considerably larger team, I had a much more evolved approach to articulating my leadership philosophy and aligning the team around a compelling vision. I even had executives far more senior than I was ask for copies of our team organizational charters so they could adopt similar approaches across their organizations.

Our approach in this book is to provide snapshots of content along with the original sources of the information. We hope you will learn from our experiences, delve further into the sources we mention, and combine them both to create the personal road map you'll use to develop the fundamentals that will help you become the executive leader you aspire to be.

BUSINESS ACUMEN

A properly developed sense of business acumen enables the creation of what we define as an executive point of view, or EPV. An EPV is the ability to assess a given situation and make a sea of information coalesce into a navigable path forward. In short, it's what you know. We disaggregate business acumen into strategic thinking, economic acumen, financial acumen, operational acumen, and market orientation.

MANAGEMENT ABILITY

A leader's ability to effectively manage execution for the delivery of results is critical to accomplishing any objective. A successful manager is skilled at assessing the current situation and setting priorities, goals, and objectives. The ability to develop tactical action plans, organize for action, and monitor implementation are other key elements of effective management.

LEADERSHIP ABILITY

Leadership is about delivering results by influencing the thoughts and actions of others. Leaders set the example and provide future-looking inspiration. They empower, they encourage, and they motivate their people to find the best way forward to accomplish their objectives. The best leaders empower groups to work together, to align around common goals, and to deliver a compelling vision.

EXECUTIVE INTELLIGENCE

When we talk about executive intelligence, we're talking about catalyzing and sustaining credibility. We see executive intelligence as sitting at the intersection of emotional intelligence and executive presence while maintaining a strong sense of what we call development awareness. We believe development awareness is the "X-factor," because it's those who are aware and determined to constantly improve who grow to their fullest potential.

PART II——DOING WHAT YOU KNOW

Executive development is a career-long journey with no final destination—there is always one more stop, something else to learn or do. You can always improve. Whether you are an aspiring executive or already an experienced one, you always have the exciting prospect of making yourself better. To help articulate our approach to executive development, we've divided the first chapter of this section into four parts.

> *Executive development is a career-long journey with no final destination.*

First, we introduce the concept of executive intuition, explain how it complements the executive point of view, and explain how you develop it. Second, we introduce what we consider the five key career transition points, how to approach them with the mindset of a CEO, and how this approach catalyzes the behaviors and habits within yourself that can be scaled at each transition point. Third, we present our approach to executive development plans, which we believe is not only an effective framework but is also fully aligned with our goal of developing scalable behaviors and habits. Finally, we outline a framework for execution and monitoring.

The most effective executives are able to empower teams and organizations to work together to deliver exceptional results. To truly become the best that you can be and develop into an exemplary executive, you've got to build well-rounded fundamentals. The fundamentals work together synergistically, and those who have mastered them also have the ability to bring out the best in others to help them achieve what they never thought was possible.

KNOWING

PART I

WHAT TO DO

CHAPTER I

BUSINESS ACUMEN

"Knowledge has to be improved, challenged, and
increased constantly, or it vanishes."

—PETER DRUCKER

Business acumen is the collective repository of all your business knowledge and experiences. It serves as the source of your ability to assess a given situation, coalesce a sea of information, and chart a navigable way forward. In other words, business acumen is what an executive point of view derives from.

It's a mistake to think an effective executive point of view can come from raw intelligence alone. Knowledge accumulated over time, combined with intelligence, can be developed into the ability to make sense of dynamic situations and translate that understanding into actionable perspectives.

A leader has to be able to think strategically and be able to understand economic, market, financial, and operational dynamics in varying contexts to know what needs to be done in any situation that may arise.

Business acumen comes from experienced-based learning—making decisions and taking actions in different situations, challenges, and contexts—but it also comes from knowledge-based learning developed through reading, thinking, and understanding.

Developing exceptional business acumen requires years of commitment to learning, applying, failing, and adapting. Through this process, a credible and sought-after executive point of view is developed. It's easy to spot someone who has it.

When I was part of a large national organization during a time of considerable challenges for our industry, one member of the executive team consistently demonstrated his exceptional business acumen. He improved employee morale and gave us all a strong sense that we would be successful, no matter what obstacles came our way. I remember one departmental all-hands meeting in which he presented his executive point of view on how we were going to move forward as a company. He was able to clearly articulate both what was similar and what was different about the current challenges relative to challenges faced historically and how our enterprise strategy was evolving as a result. Moreover, he outlined his view on which challenges were systemic and which were cyclical, and how we were evolving our operating model and financial strategy to adapt to our new environment. We all left the meeting energized and excited.

We think about business acumen as a function of five fundamentals:

1. Strategic thinking
2. Economic acumen
3. Financial acumen
4. Operational acumen
5. Market orientation

STRATEGIC THINKING

If the purpose of a business is to profitably create value for customers, then strategy is about the long-term choices that articulate how this is accomplished. Michael Porter, in his book *Competitive Strategy*, frames strategy as "deliberately choosing a different set of activities to deliver unique value." In their book *Playing to Win*, authors A. G. Lafley and Robert Martin go a step further and describe strategy as "an integrated set of five choices: a winning aspiration, where to play, how to win, core capabilities, and management systems."

Lafley and Martin define the meaning of *a winning aspiration* as the purpose and vision of your enterprise—it's who you are and what you stand for. *Where to play* tells you where your enterprise will compete—its geographies, its product categories, consumer segments, channels, and vertical stages of production. *How to win* defines your unique value proposition and the competitive advantage your enterprise will pursue. *Core capabilities* are what you need to excel given the choices being made, and *management systems* are the practices the management team implements to govern execution of the strategy.

Alan Mulally, one of America's most effective turnaround CEOs, outlines his leadership philosophy in his straightforward "Working Together Principles and Practices." One principle that is cited often is "compelling vision, comprehensive strategy, relentless implementation." Mulally demonstrates the power of going through the process of establishing a powerful vision and developing a strategy that serves as a road map outlining how the vision will be achieved; the vision and strategy give stakeholders a big-picture perspective and help them understand the interconnectedness of the enterprise. Aligning the organization around a comprehensive strategy was one of the key factors that enabled Mulally to lead Ford through a transformation that turned years of significant operating losses into sustained profitability—all the while navigating the Great Recession.

Moreover, alignment around clear strategic choices serves as the set of guardrails and filters through which all subsequent decisions are made. It aligns operational priorities, initiatives, and projects in a consistent, focused way. When an organization's decision-making, initiatives, and projects seem random and disparate, it's a clear indication that a cohesive strategy may not exist.

When we first implemented true enterprise vision-setting and strategy development, the organization we were with had been operating in pure execution mode. The executive team had been focused on "fire drills" and the immediate tasks at hand specific to their areas. This siloed operating model was leaving a lot of potential on the table. As finance leaders, we instituted a new business planning process that started with an annual strategy offsite to align the organization around a focused strategy. The attendees included not only our executive team, but all our key enterprise leaders as well. During the offsite, we set an enterprise vision, established long-term performance goals, and aligned around key strategic choices. Not only did working together in this way energize the group, but it also broke down all the preexisting departmental silos. To communicate our new strategy throughout the organization, we used posters and wallet-sized cards that articulated our vision, performance goals, and values, and distilled our strategic choices into a concise four-point plan that served as the guardrail for all subsequent planning decisions. The feedback from employees was overwhelmingly positive, and the entire executive team was aligned with the way forward—and their refreshed priorities reflected it.

ECONOMIC ACUMEN

If accounting is the language of business, economics is the framework of business, particularly in terms of managerial decision-making. Although many definitions of economics exist, Michael Baye's definition of economics as "the science of making decisions in the presence of scarce resources" is one of the more intuitive. More specifically, in *Managerial Economics and Business Strategy*, he defines managerial economics as "the study of how to direct scarce resources in the way that most efficiently achieves a managerial goal." Anyone who's gone through a corporate annual expense budgeting process would likely agree that the process of directing scarce resources to achieve company goals and objectives happens every year. Because consolidated expense budgets, more often than not, exceed what the business can afford, business unit and functional leaders have to evaluate the costs and benefits of their budget line items and make organizational trade-offs. When stakeholders are aligned and focused on the same outcomes, the process works effectively to prioritize where dollars are allocated.

In his book *Executive Economics*, Shlomo Maital explains, "Business decisions are built on three pillars—cost, value, and price," and "the job of managers is to build and run businesses by selling goods and services that provide value at a reasonable price for their customers at an acceptable cost to the business. If managers create more value at lower cost than their competitors, their businesses prosper and profit."

Cost, value, and pricing decisions can be considerably improved in any enterprise with the application of a few straightforward foundational principles of economics. Here are a few examples:

SUPPLY AND DEMAND

One of the most foundational decisions you'll have to make as a business manager is how much of a given product or service to supply to a market. If you supply too much relative to market demand, your business will become inefficient. It will also be less profitable due to the associated costs and the need to reduce prices. If you supply too little relative to market demand, your business will be forced to forego sales opportunities, and you will risk upsetting your customers.

When Ford's CEO Alan Mulally outlined his One Ford plan to turn around the struggling business in 2006, his first pillar was to "aggressively restructure to operate profitably at the current demand and changing model mix."[1] Put simply, he wanted to make enough cars to satisfy demand but not fill dealers' lots with months of excess inventory. Additionally, a leader must understand demand elasticity when making pricing decisions. For example, if you lower prices, does the increase in volume provide enough benefit to offset the lost sales dollars from the lower prices?

---

[1] Bryce Hoffman, *American Icon: Alan Mulally and the Fight to Save Ford Motor Company* (New York: Crown Business, 2012).

ECONOMIC VS. ACCOUNTING PROFIT

When you are confronted with the need to decide whether to pursue a specific initiative, it may seem appealing to rely on simple accounting profit. But *economic* profit considers the implicit opportunity costs that can often be overlooked. Looking at decisions through the lens of economic profit and opportunity costs will lead to outcomes that do a better job of allocating your resources to the opportunities with the most efficient rates of return.

I remember one conversation with a key business leader. We were reviewing our historical financial statements, and he seemed surprisingly accepting of single-digit net profitability. In the context of our industry, which had been facing considerable challenges, I generally understood why he was satisfied with the fact that we were still, at the very least, making money. But then I explained to him that if we simply sold all the assets on our balance sheet and reinvested those proceeds in the stock market (which arguably would be less risky than operating as a going concern in our industry), we'd more than double the profit dollars we were currently generating. This was an oversimplified scenario, but he immediately got the point that, given our invested capital and the riskiness of our business, we needed to generate more profitability to justify staying in the business. In other words, that simple example got him thinking about opportunity costs and economic profit, without me having to brush the dust off my economics textbooks.

INCENTIVES

The ability to structure incentive programs around specific desired outcomes is one of the most critical managerial skills a leader might be called upon to use. Incentives considerably influence what your employees are working on and how hard they are working. When you, as a manager, combine the right goals, objectives, and incentives, work will get done effectively and efficiently.

When we wanted to improve our inventory management at a retailer I was working for, our first point of focus was to create the right incentive compensation program within our merchandising organization. Because our business had both high-turn, low-margin products and low-turn, high-margin products, we established an incentive compensation program using Gross Margin Return on Inventory as the primary bonus measure. For non-retailers, GMROI is a metric that levels the playing field across product categories with different economics. In other words, GMROI targets can be achieved by managing sales and inventory levels, gross margin, or a combination of both. Not surprisingly, once we instituted this change and set product GMROI goals, our buyers for our low-margin product categories started managing inventory levels much more strictly and began to hit their GMROI targets. This freed up millions of dollars of working capital that had been tied up in inventory, which made a big difference for our business.

MARGINAL ANALYSIS

One key component you'll want to consider when constructing a business case is marginal analysis. This involves evaluating the trade-offs in terms of the incremental benefit vs. the incremental costs of a decision.

For example, while working for a large organization, I led a team that evaluated the efficacy of our customer loyalty program. The program had become increasingly large and expensive, and we wanted to ensure that it was optimized to drive the maximum value in incremental sales with the lowest possible incremental expense. Customers joining the loyalty program received a co-branded credit card to make purchases. To understand incremental program sales, we had to find a way to differentiate between sales that would have happened anyway, just with another payment type, and sales that were truly incremental and a direct result of being a member of the program. Our analytics team used a method that allowed us to match loyalty customers with non-loyalty customers to compare spend levels over time. Customers with nearly identical characteristics (e.g., spend levels, age, demographics, etc.) were paired. The only difference was that one was a loyalty customer and one was not. As a control, we looked at spend levels of matched customers prior to the point when one became a loyalty member; not surprisingly, they were nearly the same. We then compared the spend levels after one became a loyalty member and considered the difference in spend levels to be incremental. This wasn't a perfect methodology; it was merely a way to estimate incremental program benefits so we could evolve the program and improve ROI.

COMPARATIVE ADVANTAGE

One of the most important decisions you'll have to make as a manager is deciding what you'll do in-house and what you will outsource. Understanding comparative advantage means understanding what capabilities should be outsourced, because the opportunity cost of doing them in-house is too high, or the quality of the in-house work is too low, or some combination of both factors.

While I was the financial leader of one company, we made the decision to outsource a considerable portion of our accounting operations. During the final sales call with the firm that would eventually become our outsource partner, the sales team focused almost exclusively on our expense savings if we chose to work with them. The savings were great, but I was sold after their implementation director walked me through their operating model, processes, and procedures. They had developed a process so effective and efficient that we would never have been able to replicate it internally without spending significantly more than we were spending at the time. Making this move allowed us to leverage the comparative advantage of our accounting operations outsource partner and reinvest the savings to build out other more strategic functions internally. These decisions allowed us to position the finance team as a strategic partner with key stakeholders and add a lot more value to the business.

FINANCIAL ACUMEN

In their book *Financial Intelligence*, authors Karen Berman, Joe Knight, and John Case state, "The art of accounting and finance is the art of using limited data to come as close as possible to an accurate description of how well a company is performing." The key here is to understand what's behind all the numbers. Well-constructed financial plans and budgets reflect all the planned strategic and operational decisions and expected outcomes of the business. When compared with actual financial results, the planned vs. actual variances serve as a primary tool to understand what's going on in your business, what's working, and what's not. Because financial plans reflect everything you think is going to happen in the business (key decisions, upcoming initiatives, market trends, competitive changes, etc.) and actual financial results reflect everything that actually happened in the business, there is seldom better scorecard for measuring business outcomes.

CASH AND CASH FLOW

Cash pays the bills, so it's not surprising a lack of cash is the primary driver of business failure. Kevin Cope discusses this concept in *Seeing the Big Picture: Business Acumen to Build Your Credibility, Career, and Company*. The business's cash position (cash on hand) and liquidity (ability to turn non-cash assets into cash quickly) are key factors in assessing how solvent the business is. The cash flow statement outlines the three key activities generating and using cash, and forecasting these statements can help you

(continued)

understand how your cash position is expected to change over time. To summarize:

- Operating cash flow is the cash generated and used in core operations of the business.
- Investing cash flow is the cash generated and used in the buying and selling of assets.
- Financing cash flow is the cash generated and used in receiving or paying back debt, issuing or buying back stock, and paying dividends.

PROFIT AND LOSS

An income statement reflects business performance in terms of the business's ability to generate profit. Trends in revenue growth, profit dollars, and margins can be quickly analyzed by comparing historical results. The authors of *Financial Intelligence* explain that "it's the accountants' best effort to show the sales the company generated during a given time period, the costs incurred in making those sales (including the costs of operating the business for that span of time), and the profit, if any, that is left over." Accruals and allocations are examples of the accountants' attempt to book revenues or expenses in the time period earned or incurred and assign them to the responsible business unit so that executives can better understand the performance of their area of responsibility and make informed decisions.

THE BALANCE SHEET

The balance sheet is the place to look when you want to understand the health of your business at any given time. It outlines your company's assets (what's owned by the business), the liabilities (what's owed by the business), and the equity (the difference between the two). While the income statement accounts for the business performance over a specific period of time, the balance sheet is a culmination of the business's performance (and, of course, the financing and investment activities) since your business was formed. The company's solvency (its ability to cover liabilities with assets), its ability to grow equity over time, and its ability to weather an economic downturn are only a few examples of what can be analyzed from the balance sheet.

TIME VALUE OF MONEY AND ROI

Tim Koller, Marc Goedhart, and David Wessels put forth in their book *Valuation*, "The guiding principle of business value creation is a refreshingly simple construct: companies that grow and earn a return on capital that exceeds their cost of capital create value." At the heart of any investment decision is understanding its NPV (net present value) and/or IRR (internal rate of return). The former is the discounted present value of all future expected cash flows with the time value of money a foundational component of the calculation. In essence, the time value of money states that a dollar next year is worth less than a dollar today, because the

(continued)

opportunity cost of investing today's dollar and earning a return over that time period is subtracted from the value of next year's dollar. When you compare the NPV of two competing projects or initiatives, you can determine which is expected to generate more value. Similarly, return on investment (commonly measured by IRR) can be used to compare competing decisions and can be compared relative to the cost of capital employed. When the return on invested capital exceeds the cost of capital, value is created, and vice versa.

OPERATIONAL ACUMEN

Operational acumen refers to understanding the interconnectedness of the business functions, the business's capabilities, and the processes by which the business converts inputs to value-added products and services. If execution is the result of thousands of decisions made every day by employees acting on the information they have, then success depends on the company's ability to coordinate these decisions in a way that delivers value efficiently.

To move from planning to execution, executives must develop the right operational principles and practices. At one organization, we were asked to lead a turnaround of their merchandising group. It was clear from day one that changing the dynamics of the team was going to be a significant challenge. Decision rights were unclear and ungoverned, team members were not being held accountable for their performance, buying decisions were driven by instinct rather than by data-driven insights, and the group lacked foresight and failed to consider the level of risk the company was taking on by these actions. Even at the tactical level, buyers were plagued by conflicting directions, lack of management systems and controls, and overwhelming ambiguity with respect to their roles. The only way the group was going to improve was to fundamentally evolve their operating principles. We focused on four key areas: Operating Model, Organizational Structure, Governance, and Capabilities.

OPERATING MODEL

The operating model is about understanding the processes that convert inputs to outputs, workplace design, and information distribution. Although organizations can evolve to better models, the process can be a daunting one that often leads to unintended consequences. The evolution or creation of a new operating model must start with a proper assessment of the current state and is followed by a clear articulation of the desired operational outcomes. From there, the key is to develop a model that will effectively allow the business to close the gaps between current and desired states and provide an environment for collaborative communication and information sharing.

When we evolved the operating model for the merchandising group, we started the process by clearly mapping out each stage of the buyer workflow at the most detailed level. We developed process flowcharts that clearly outlined each stage in the process of converting inputs to outputs. We then layered in historical productivity and performance metrics to better understand the parts of the process that were working. This also enabled us to quickly identify gaps that were negatively impacting throughput. From there, we acquired the necessary information from key operators about why the gaps existed, and we developed new goals to use in the model. The final design was formulated by simulating various models and iterating an approach that would alleviate the current issues, while simultaneously ensuring there were no disruptions to other functional areas.

ORGANIZATIONAL STRUCTURE

Organizational structure refers to how you organize your people in a way that allows them to understand their roles, responsibilities, and decision rights. The structure also allows organizational leaders to accurately assess talent. Ineffective organizational structures often lead to what we refer to as "dupli-siloing," which indicates both duplicated and siloed workstreams. This will always result in lower throughput, increased costs, and process bottlenecks. Designing a structure that empowers people prevents these types of roadblocks and encourages value-added actions.

In the example of the merchandising group turnaround, one thing was clear: Many of the responsibilities and decision rights were heavily weighted to a handful of people, many of whom gave conflicting, duplicative, and ambiguous direction. The new organizational structure that was put in place appropriately distributed responsibilities and decision rights across the function, which led to a more collaborative and efficient environment where stakeholders were fully empowered.

GOVERNANCE

When the right management systems are put in place, you instill a culture of accountability. There are many examples of organizations that lack the ability to hold people accountable for the progress they've made with respect to their planned goals and objectives. We believe the most effective form of governance comes through the utilization of business and functional reviews. These are meetings that are held on a regular schedule where all key stakeholders come together to review performance, progress on key initiatives, and special-attention items that require people to work together and solve problems.

When we executed the new merchandising operating model, a key part of it was the institution of weekly functional reviews. This provided a chance for all levels of the merchandising team to come together to ensure that targets were being met, progress was being made on merchandising priorities, and any issues encountered were addressed. This created a forum for all members of the merchandising group to be held accountable for their areas of responsibility and to solve challenges together.

CAPABILITIES

Capabilities refer to evolving capability requirements like technology or tools that support the new operating model, governance, and organizational structure. With our merchandising turnaround, we developed a merchandising platform that took our inventory planning and analysis to the next level. We were able to produce "buyer guidebooks" that informed performance-based open-to-buy recommendations based on facts and data. This capability empowered our buyers to focus on buying great products with the real-time information to course-correct as needed.

In his book *State of Readiness*, Joseph F. Paris Jr. asserts that the competitive advantages of companies lie in their ability to quicken their vision-building and strategy-execution efforts by identifying challenges quickly and accelerating decision-making so they are able to formulate and deploy responses with greater agility. He asserts that a company's commitment to building a culture of continuous improvement is the foundation to achieving operational excellence—which is the capability and situational awareness attained when the enterprise can align itself to pursue its strategies. Our relentless focus on process and the people who manage it will allow you to build competitive advantages within your organization. Despite the challenges, the new operating model we put in place for the merchandising group transformed our merchandising efficiency and effectiveness. The result was better sales performance and far greater inventory management.

MARKET ORIENTATION

When we talk about market orientation, we are talking about making a focused effort to meet customers' needs—rather than selling them products or services. The Blockbuster failure is a great example of a business that was too focused on the products it sold. Blockbuster's core product offering was rental movies; for most of its existence, this met the demands of the market—a large selection of conveniently consumed media entertainment. Had Blockbuster truly focused on what the market was demanding, it would have realized both "selection" and "convenience" were being rapidly redefined. Movies were starting to become a smaller and smaller share of the available media consumers could entertain themselves with, and instead of having to go to a brick-and-mortar location, customers could have DVDs mailed to them. It wasn't long before convenience went a step further and customers could seamlessly download movies right from their couches—needing nothing more than a remote control. Growing up, I was in Blockbuster nearly every week, and the only adaptation I can recall was when they shifted from videotapes to DVDs.

As Theodore Levitt illustrates by example in *Marketing Myopia*, "The railroads are in trouble today not because the need was filled by others (cars, trucks, airplanes, even telephones), but because it was not filled by the railroads themselves. They let others take customers away from them because they assumed themselves to be in the railroad business rather than in the transportation business." This example concisely illustrates the importance of market orientation vs. product orientation: The former is always evolving and adapting the business to meet the needs of paying customers—it's not just "selling what we make."

Shifting to a market orientation starts by looking externally. As a guiding framework, Michael Porter's Five Forces concept from his book *Competitive Strategy* is a great place to start, given it outlines the primary forces that drive competition within any particular industry. Porter lists the five forces as the potential threat of new entrants, the power of suppliers, the power of buyers, the threat of substitutes, and industry competition. Moreover, Porter considers customers, suppliers, substitutes, and potential entrants all as "competitors" within an industry with "all five competitive forces jointly [determining] the intensity of industry competition and profitability." I saw firsthand the intense power of suppliers when I joined a retailer in a huge but highly fragmented industry. This fragmented retail industry was supplied by much more consolidated industry behemoths that had far greater brand recognition among the final consumers. As a result, our suppliers had tremendous say in many aspects of our business—from store design to marketing strategy to customer service. Consequently, our long-term strategic planning was focused on diversifying our business in a way that reduced some of the supplier power, giving us more control over our future.

Market orientation begins with understanding and serving the needs and wants of customers. It also involves understanding the dynamics and interconnectedness of all competitive forces within an industry. It forms a foundational component to developing a strategy that creates value for your customers in a way that's profitable for your business.

BUSINESS ACUMEN GTR ACTION PLAN

Practice makes perfect. Successful athletes, scholars, and leaders take the time to train, study, and continually challenge themselves to exceed their own expectations. They train the muscles that will lay the foundation for their success.

We designed GTR ("Get the Reps") action plans to provide a series of tactical action steps that can help professionals take ownership of their executive fundamentals development. Using them is similar to hiring a trainer to craft a workout plan. They are structured in a four-phase process: Plan, Learn, Practice, Measure (PLPM). The first phase involves building out a comprehensive plan that maps out the actions you plan to take to develop specific areas of your fundamentals. The second phase involves acquiring knowledge and information about the area of executive fundamentals that requires development. The third phase deals with practicing and applying the knowledge and information you have learned, and the last phase measures your progress. Each GTR action plan includes examples of action items for each phase.

BUSINESS ACUMEN GTR ("GET THE REPS") ACTION PLAN

PLAN

- Undergo a current-state assessment of your business acumen to identify your strengths and areas for development
- Devise a comprehensive plan tailored to addressing your areas of development; the development plan should include:
  - A checklist of tasks that you plan to complete to learn, practice, and measure your progress in developing your business acumen
  - A list of reading materials, books, and resources that target your development areas

LEARN

- Subscribe to recurring business periodicals, forums, e-magazines, newsletters, blogs, and research studies

- Each year, develop a comprehensive reading list
- Identify, network, and engage with key executives and industry leaders
- Receive formalized training or consider executive education to learn specific areas of business
- Sign up to attend relevant conferences
- Observe and document how leaders within your company interact, behave, and share their perspectives on the business

PRACTICE

- Proactively volunteer to participate in new projects that provide an opportunity outside of your core realm of responsibility and understanding
- Find time to offer up new ideas and solutions to pressing business challenges on projects that you are currently on or projects that you are aware of; take the opportunity in meetings to offer up ideas based on data-driven insights or learning from your experience
- Actively listen to everyone's perspective in meetings and look to understand their point of view
- Develop your voice by proactively participating during meetings with your own perspective from your learning

MEASURE

- Observe the evolution of your EPV
- Request feedback from mentors, direct and skip-level managers, and peers to assess your progress in developing your business acumen
- Track your small "wins" by measuring the number of opportunities where you were able to confidently express your EPV
- Evaluate your progress and adjust your plan based on feedback
- Complete the Business Acumen section of the Executive Fundamentals Self-Assessment

CHAPTER 2

MANAGEMENT ABILITY

"Leadership complements management; it doesn't replace it."

—JOHN P. KOTTER

The ability of every leader to effectively manage execution for the delivery of results is critical to accomplishing any objective, regardless of its nature. When we assess the current state of our business; when we set priorities, goals, and objectives; and when we develop tactical action plans, organize for action, and measure progress, we are engaging in the key elements of effective management.

In *The Practice of Management,* Peter Drucker distills the concept of management into three major functions—functions that he says must be balanced and harmonized. He sees these functions as managing a business, managing managers, and managing workers and work.

In this book, we are going to approach these points in reverse order, since they are exactly the key career transition points that most people experience on their way to the executive ranks. Early in our career, we're busy managing only our own tasks and work; later, with success and mastery of our jobs, we accept responsibility for managing other individual workers. When we are acknowledged to have been successful with both of these roles, we begin to manage managers. And finally, once we have a track record of managing all three, we move to the management of a function or a business. Although the fundamentals of effective management are essentially the same at each stage, the role that an executive (or an aspiring executive) plays in the management process must evolve at each step. Managers of individuals clearly must be responsible for managing the entire work-flow process. And although executives are accountable for managing the process, the key to shared success will always stem from granting others the power they need to manage and execute the delivery of the results for which they're responsible. In other words, a successful executive will know how (and be willing) to delegate responsibility and decision rights, as well as know how to structure the right work environment and management systems to ensure that the work is getting done.

Great managers are capable of assessing the current state so that they understand all the factors at play. They work with cross-functional stakeholders to understand organizational priorities, and they align the priorities of the team they directly manage with the broader organizational priorities. With priorities established, they empower their teams to develop detailed action plans outlining how priority goals and objectives will be delivered. They remove obstacles and enable team members to implement their plans. Finally, they put in place the practices and systems to monitor execution so that adjustments and course-corrections can be made.

The five fundamentals of management are as follows:

1. Situational Assessment
2. Setting Priorities
3. Comprehensive Planning
4. Organizing for Action
5. Monitoring Implementation

SITUATIONAL ASSESSMENT

Any of us who has ever walked into a new situation knows that being able to understand the current realities facing the business—both from internal and external perspectives—is a critical starting point if we are to achieve success.

To better understand the realities from an internal perspective, we generally find it helpful to construct an evaluation framework that is built around the idea of the five Ps: performance, people, product, process, and pace. In other words, business performance can be thought of as a function of its people, its products, its processes, and its pace of progress. Leveraging this framework was particularly helpful in understanding the baseline situation in one organizational turnaround we led. From a product perspective, the company had become completely reliant on historical offerings that had become commoditized and low margin. There wasn't much of a focused pricing or marketing strategy, either. Organized processes were almost nonexistent. At best, execution could have been described as organized chaos. From a people perspective, significant talent gaps were present at all levels. There was no HR function, and the culture had become dysfunctional with low employee engagement and morale. Finally, the pace of progress was hardly noticeable. There was limited appetite for change among the executive team, and progress on initiatives was unfocused and stalled. Clearly, there were a lot of issues, but utilizing this framework allowed us to isolate the most pressing needs and begin to develop change plans in a way that was organized and made sense to the employees.

When you decide it's time to size up a situation from an internal perspective, incorporate the following key assessment areas into your framework.

INTERNAL SITUATION ASSESSMENT AREAS

PERFORMANCE

Business performance is ultimately reflected in the organization's ability to generate and sustain growth, profitability, and cash flow. Evaluating historical financial statements to understand trends, particularly against established goals and plans, can build considerable context into how the business has been performing. It's also important to understand whether performance goals have been established, what the established measures are, and what the gaps are between goaled and actual performance.

PEOPLE

People are the most important asset in any organization, and employee engagement, morale, and talent will have significant impacts on overall performance. Key assessment areas include culture, talent, and structure. To understand the existing culture, it's helpful to complete a thorough review of any available employee engagement surveys; develop stakeholder maps; complete cross-functional interviews; and review the organizational structure, roles, responsibilities, and decision rights. To understand the existing levels of talent, it's helpful to review any available performance reviews, in addition to conducting interviews with people managers and HR personnel. Finally, evaluating and understanding existing incentive plans and the impact on behaviors is important.

PRODUCT

Product decisions are what determine whether or not the business is creating value for customers. To build baseline context, it's helpful to review target customer segments, the product or service portfolio, mix strategies, pricing and marketing strategies, and individual product or service value propositions. Evaluating individual product or service growth and profitability trends with industry and competitive benchmarks can provide great perspective into what the market demand is and whether customer value creation is expanding or contracting.

PROCESS

The process is about how effectively and efficiently the business is operating, which impacts not only the level of value that can be created for customers, but also the level of value captured for the business. Simply put, the process is how inputs are procured and converted into salable outputs. It's helpful to map and evaluate the existing operating model and process flow charts, workplace design, and distribution of information. Cross-functional stakeholder interviews can also serve as a useful way to understand key challenges and bottlenecks that can serve as initial focus areas.

PACE

Pace is really about the rate of progress in terms of both progress on key initiatives and evolving and innovating to build a sustainable business for tomorrow. Key assessment areas include the mix of new vs. legacy products or services, new product or service development, new business investment, and new growth or distribution channels. Equally important is understanding the organization's change capacity and ability to execute strategic and operational initiatives. The competition is always moving forward, and if your business is being conducted virtually the same today as it was years ago, there's a good chance you're being left behind.

From an external perspective, understanding the macroeconomic and industry influences that affect your organization is crucial to understanding why your business is performing the way it is. In terms of macroeconomic influences, understanding where you are in the business cycle, GDP growth trends, interest rates, access to credit, inflation, and unemployment rates are only a few of the key areas to be aware of.

As a new manager, it's essential that you begin to comprehend external forces by building a macroeconomic context that will help you understand why the industry dynamics are what they are. In terms of industry influences, authors Craig Fleisher and Babette Bensoussan offer concise information. In *Business and Competitive Analysis,* they explain, "Intelligence about customers, competitors, potential partners, suppliers, and other influential stakeholders is a company's first, and often only, line of offense/defense."

Accordingly, it's for this reason that we always start our executive team business reviews with a section called "External Trends and Developments." In this section of the review, we cover any new external information that could affect our business. Specifically, we're looking at key macroeconomic indicators, industry performance, competitive and vendor earnings releases, etc. Having a regular review of new external information helps prevent our team from becoming too insular, and it gives us important context that allows us to evolve our strategy over time.

In terms of leveraging an effective external forces framework, Porter's Five Forces and a SWOT analysis are great places to start. The former is predicated on what Porter considers the five industry forces: buyer power, supplier power, threats of substitutes, threats of new entry, and competitive rivalry. The latter considers strengths, weaknesses, opportunities, and threats. These are just two examples of effective frameworks that help organize analyses specific to the environment your business operates in.

Finally, to fully complete your analysis of external influences, it's important that you gather information on industry concentration and where your business is in relation to the industry life cycle, regulatory environment, price competition, market share trends, and competitive benchmarks.

SETTING PRIORITIES

In her book *Rise*, Patty Azzarello emphasizes the need for executives to set ruthless priorities when she states, "Simply put, highly successful people don't do everything." Whether it's annual, monthly, weekly, or daily priorities, completing a focused set of the most important action items is more effective than partially completing a much larger set of action items.

We find it helpful to think about priorities in terms of performance goals and objectives, and from a strategic and operational perspective. Annual performance goals should cascade directly from long-term performance goals, and operational objectives should cascade directly from strategic objectives. The table on the following page illustrates this framework.

Also on the following page, you will see that our "Business Planning Cascade" diagram illustrates our approach to developing comprehensive plans to achieve priority goals and objectives. It is built upon three guiding principles. First, work back from the destination. We define and align our long-term ambition and performance goals and develop a strategy that achieves both. Second, choices before projections. We align strategic and cascade and operational choices first, and then develop comprehensive financial plans that reflect those choices. Third, everyone is included in the planning process. We engage our key stakeholders to garner perspectives, and obtain alignment and buy-in.

	Strategic Priorities	Operational Priorities
Performance Goals	Long-term, recurring, "business-as-usual" goals (e.g., maintain 15% operating margin)	Short-term, recurring, "business-as-usual" goals (e.g., expand operating margin from 8% to 10% by EOY)
Objectives	Specific long-term strategic outcomes that are clear and measurable with a specific end-date (e.g., create store presence in 15 top U.S. cities within 5 years)	Specific short-term operational outcomes that are clear and measurable with a specific end-date (e.g., open stores in New York and Chicago by EOY)

BUSINESS PLANNING CASCADE

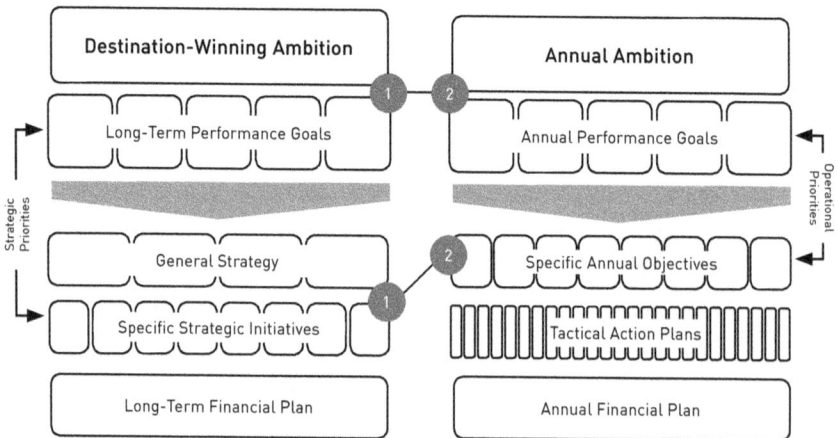

We've found this framework effective from the enterprise level down to subsegments of business units or functional departments. For example, at one organization where we leveraged this framework, we started by bringing together the executive team to define enterprise-level strategic priorities. Once the executive team was aligned, each business unit and functional leader was responsible for cascading enterprise priorities into operational priorities for their specific areas.

In other situations where enterprise priorities were not clear, we've leveraged the same framework paired with a philosophy we call *Define and Align*. For example, while I was serving as the leader of a small functional department, neither enterprise nor functional priorities were clear. Despite the absence of clear direction from those who were senior to me, I worked together with my direct reports to define our team's top five priorities. Then, I aligned with key stakeholders to ensure we were working toward the same outcomes. Additionally, we provided regular progress reports throughout the year to remind stakeholders of what we were focused on and how we were doing.

This process is only effective when you proactively own defining your top priorities and then align through an iterative process with key stakeholders (in particular, your boss) before implementation begins. It's also important to include your direct reports in the process, so their perspectives are heard and incorporated, increasing ownership and commitment from those who will ultimately be responsible for carrying out the work. If there's one takeaway from the idea of Define and Align, it's to not wait for priorities to be set for you.

Setting priorities is as simple as defining and limiting the desired outcomes from the start. This way, we've got the best chance to fully deliver what's most important to the organization.

COMPREHENSIVE PLANNING

Once we know where we're going, our next step should be to develop the action plans we will use to achieve whatever our intended operational performance goals and objectives are. For example, if our annual performance goal is to increase operating margin from 8 to 10 percent, the tactical action plan outlines all of the individual tasks and associated timelines and responsibilities required to achieve the goal.

In his book *Pleased But Not Satisfied*, David Sokol outlines a simple acronym to achieve goals and objectives: PEMC. It stands for Plan, Execute, Measure, Correct. What he's saying is, if we start by developing a comprehensive plan, we facilitate a greater ability to execute. If we then measure actual outcomes relative to planned outcomes, we can effectively monitor our performance and course-correct if we start to get off track.

Just as when you cascade strategic priorities into operational priorities, tactical action plans are the next step in the process—that's where operational priorities are cascaded into specific action items.

EMPOWERING DIRECT REPORTS

An important step in comprehensive planning is to empower your direct reports and their teams to develop the tactical action plans you'll need. George S. Patton Jr., the infamous WWII general, was quoted saying, "Never tell people how to do things. Tell them what to do, and they will surprise you with their ingenuity." This quote concisely captures the essence of how to empower people. Help them determine the *what*, and give them the freedom to figure out the *how*.

Every year when setting annual priorities for my specific areas of responsibility, I start by including my direct reports in the process of determining our priority goals and objectives. I do this because I very much value their perspectives and because I want to increase their level of buy-in to what we're focusing on. As part of this process, each priority has a single direct report who will take responsibility for ensuring the goal or objective is delivered. I leave it completely to that individual to work with their team and peers to develop the tactical action plans. Although I do review the action plans before finalizing them, I only get involved in plan development when I'm asked to do so.

I have found this to be a simple but effective approach to empowering employees. By delegating responsibility and some of the decision rights, employees feel a much greater sense of ownership. It's also important to remember there are many ways to achieve a specific objective. But what's most important in any situation is that the objective is fully achieved *on* or *ahead of* schedule. What's less important is the *way* in which it is achieved.

ACHIEVING SPECIFIC OUTCOMES

The process of achieving outcomes is as simple as breaking goals and objectives into smaller and smaller pieces. For example, the enterprise may have three key strategic objectives that could be considered the business's strategy or its strategic plan. Those three strategic objectives might cascade into nine operational objectives that could be considered the operational plan. Each of those nine operational objectives might then cascade into fifteen action items that could be considered the tactical action plan for each particular objective, and so on.

Finally, the outputs of this process should serve as inputs into the financial planning process. This way, all choices, decisions, and planned outcomes will be reflected in long-term and annual financial plans, enabling the measurement and control of progress throughout the upcoming year.

ORGANIZING FOR ACTION

The key to organizing for effective action is to implement an effective team structure and to align around roles, responsibilities, and decision rights. Team structure should be a function of the organization's strategy and should be aligned with the stakeholders served, whether internal or external. A great place to start is by outlining the team operating model—or how the team will work together to support the overall strategy and serve constituencies. In the book *Principles of General Management*, written by John Colley Jr. and colleagues, the authors state, "A fundamental purpose of an organizational structure is to define the authority relationships and related responsibilities in an organization in order to establish the chain of command. The resulting 'structure' permits effective control and accountability." They go on to say, "For companies to be successful, the supporting infrastructure, systems, and culture must also align with management's strategy."

CREATING AN OPERATING MODEL

Outlining the team operating model at the start allows for a more effective organizational hierarchy. To map a team operating model, we've found the following framework helpful:

Start by defining how the team creates value for customers, whether they are internal or external. This includes defining team competencies (what we know), capabilities (what we do), and value proposition (what we produce).

Next, define where the team delivers value to internal or external customers. This includes distribution channels, which, again, can be internal if we're talking about the operating model of a functional department (e.g., marketing, HR, finance, etc.).

Finally, define how the team captures value for the business.

CREATING AN ORGANIZATIONAL STRUCTURE

Defining roles, responsibilities, and decision rights for all the team members in your particular setting is critical to avoiding confusion over who's responsible for what.

A standard starting point is for a leader to leverage the RACI matrix. Its purpose is to list who's responsible, who's accountable, who's consulted, and who's informed. "Responsible" denotes the individual who ensures that the work is completed. "Accountable" denotes the individual who has overall accountability for the individual that is responsible. "Consulted" denotes stakeholders who contribute to getting the work done, whether through thought or action. "Informed" denotes stakeholders who are simply provided updates regarding the work being done.

See the following example with the team's recurring responsibilities and deliverables on the y-axis, and the team members and stakeholders on the x-axis.

Team Responsibilities	Our Team					Stakeholders			
	Person A	Person B	Person C	Person D	Person E	CEO	COO	CFO	VP
Responsibility A									
Responsibility 1	I	R	C	C	C	I	I	I	I
Responsibility 2	I	R	C	C	C	I	I	I	I
Responsibility B									
Responsibility 1	I	I	I	A	R	C	C	I	I
Responsibility 2	I	C	I	A	R	I	I	I	I
Responsibility 3	I	A	I	C	R	C	C	I	C
Responsibility 4	I	A	I		R	C	C	I	I

BUSINESS PERFORMANCE REVIEW SCORECARD

ENTERPRISE

1   Our Ambition

Our Mission: We are the intersection of great food and great for you

Our Vision: To be the #1 Korean-inspired fast casual destination in the United States

2   Our Strategy

[1] Develop 'recipe-simple, taste-complex' menu that's as nutritious as delicious

[2] Deliver best-in-class experience through immaculately kept stores and fast service

[3] Develop efficient, scalable and replicable operations platform

3   Enterprise Priorities   John (CEO)

2018 PERFORMANCE GOALS	PLAN	FCST
[1] Customers Served (M)	5.0	4.8
[2] 2018 Revenue ($M)	700.1	710.5
[3] Gross Margin (%)	60.1	62.9
[4] Operating Margin (%)	10.0	13.9
[5] New Client Revenue (%)	40.0	38.4

2018 OBJECTIVES	AE	STATUS
[1] National Rollout of refreshed menu (6/15)	JJ	G
[2] Three new store openings in Northeast (9/15)	JS	G
[3] Refresh of Midwest stores (8/15)	SH	Y
[4] Develop franchise platform (12/15)	JH	G
[5] Five store test of new operating model (9/15)	VH	G

4   Financial Performance Summary

ENTERPRISE P&L ($M)–MAR	YTD ACTUAL	YTD PLAN	B/(W) $ Δ	B/(W) % Δ
Revenue	76.0	86.2	(10.2)	-12%
COR	16.1	32.8	16.7	51%
Gross Profit	59.9	53.3	6.6	12%
GM%	78.8%	61.9%	bps	1,690
Operating Expense	56.7	56.8	0.1	0%
Operating Profit	3.2	(35)	6.7	39.3%
OM%	4.2%	-4.0%	bps	825

5   Business Segment Priorities

[a] Northeast Region

[b] Southeast Region

[d] Northwest Region

[e] Midwest Region

[f] Franchise

6   Business Function Priorities

[a] Sales & Marketing

[b] Human Resources

[d] Corporate Finance

[e] Information Technology

[f] Supply Chain

7   Performance / ...

BUSINESS/FUNCTION
Northwest Region
Corporate Finance
Supply Chain

BUSINESS/FUNCTION
Corporate Finance
Northwest Region

BUSINESS SEGMENTS & FUNCTIONS

	2018 PG-Status	2018 O-Status	Key Updates
Jeff (VP)	1.0	0.6	[1] New district managers hired [2] Slight delay in this year's key initiatives
Judy (VP)	0.2	0.9	[1] Weather related store closure hurt performance [2] All initiatives on-track
Karen (VP) SAR	-0.8	0.9	[1] Construction project causing store traffic issues [2] Developing contingency plan
Sarah (VP)	0.4	0.5	[1] Lost key managers to competitors [2] Slight delays in this year's key initiatives
James (VP)	1.0	0.8	[1] Franchise business case approved, plans developed [2] On-track to add five franchisees this year

	2018 PG-Status	2018 O-Status	Key Updates
Gordon (CMO)	0.7	0.6	[1] New sales executive hired [2] Exploring outsource sales model to augment team
Oliver (CPO)	0.8	1.0	[1] Talent acquisition capability under development [2] Achieved YTD recruitment goals
Megan (CFO) SAR	1.0	0.5	[1] Lost several key equity investors for series C funding [2] Exploring cost-benefit of debt vs. equity raise
Rhonda (CTO)	1.0	1.0	[1] ERP migration underway and on track [2] Data breach security platform went live and is performing well
Tim (CSO) SAR	0.6	-0.4	[1] New contingency supplier plan off-track [2] Starting to achieve partial targeted savings

SPECIAL ATTENTION REVIEW

Initiatives At-Risk & Opportunities

RISK	SITUATION	GOAL/OBJECTIVE/ACTION	AE/R	STATUS
Performance Risk– 2018 Revenue	Customer traffic has been soft due to adjacent construction project	Expand delivery options	Jeff/Alex	On-track
Initiative Risk– 2018 Capital Raise	Several key investor dropped out of series C funding round	Identify new investors to achieve target raise	Megan/Kayla	Plan WIP
Initiative Risk– 2018 OpEx savings	SC 2.0 platform delayed due to budget cuts	Identify savings to refund program	Tim/Randy	No Plan Yet

OPPORTUNITY	SITUATION	GOAL/OBJECTIVE/ACTION	AE/R	STATUS
Financing	Obtained preliminary approval for $100M debt financing	Evaluate cost-benefit of incremental debt vs. equity raise	Megan/Kayla	Plan WIP
2019 Revenue	Approached to purchase four store chain in Seattle	Evaluate cost-benefit of acquisition and fit with existing store platform	Karen/Jean	Plan WIP

The grid you've created should identify what role each individual plays for each specific responsibility and/or deliverable. With an effective team operating model; clear organizational structure; and a clear outline of roles, responsibilities, and deliverables, your team will be ready to begin execution.

MONITORING IMPLEMENTATION

In late 2006, Alan Mulally was appointed CEO of Ford Motor Company to lead what would become one of the greatest corporate turnarounds in American business history. The cornerstone of his management philosophy was what he called his BPR process, or the business plan review. The business plan review was a weekly meeting that all executives were required to attend; at each meeting, the executives were required to provide status updates with respect to their areas of responsibility. Executives were required to personally present their performance and progress updates, which emphasized accountability. He adamantly believed that "everyone knows the plan, the status, and the areas that need special attention." This simple process was a key ingredient in changing the corporate culture to one in which clear accountability was fostered and where everyone worked together to achieve common goals and objectives.

Following Mulally's example, we have utilized the business review process as our primary tool for monitoring implementation of our business plans with much success. For example, at one organization in need of transformation, we launched weekly business reviews and almost immediately experienced a shift to an accountability culture. Before the weekly business reviews were instituted, goals were set and forgotten, and executives rarely met, which created organizational silos. After we launched the weekly business reviews, everyone became accountable for presenting performance and progress for their areas of responsibility. We set the example in how we presented our specific areas of responsibility and leveraged easily digestible scorecards (like the example on page 49) to communicate progress.

With respect to our performance goals, we always presented great detail about what we were planning to do when underperforming. When it came to our initiatives, we clearly outlined both the milestones we had delivered and the upcoming milestones. It didn't take long for other executives to follow suit and come equally prepared with their own scorecards.

Monitoring implementation through a business or functional review is a critical practice that ensures the execution that is taking place is achieving planned outcomes and provides the information to course-correct when needed.

BUSINESS REVIEW

An effective business review should be scheduled as a recurring meeting with all accountable stakeholders in attendance. A clear and consistent agenda is essential. Whether you're the CEO of a multi-billion-dollar corporation or a project manager of a small team, the process and agenda is built on the same foundation. Here is an example agenda for an enterprise business review:

Agenda	Driver	Time
1. External Trends & Developments		8:00-8:30
a. Macroeconomic Updates b. Industry Updates c. Competitive Updates d. Customer/Supplier Updates	CEO	
2. Enterprise Review		8:30-9:30
a. Strategic Review b. Operational Review c. Financial Review	CEO COO CFO	
3. Business-Unit Review		9:45-10:30
a. Store Operations b. Online Operations c. Wholesale Operations	EVP, Stores EVP, eCommerce EVP, Products Group	
4. Functional Review		10:30-12:00
a. Sales & Marketing b. Merchandising c. Supply Chain d. Technology e. HR f. Finance	CCO CMO EVP, Supply Chain CTO CHRO CFO	
5. Special Attention Review		12:15-1:00
a. At-Risk Performance b. At-Risk Initiatives c. Emerging Opportunities d. Business Cases, Insights & Recommendations	CEO	

In the first section of this agenda, we've always found it helpful to start with an external perspective so we can maintain awareness of what's going on around us. The second section is focused on our enterprise-level priorities and financial performance. The third and fourth sections are where responsibility center owners (e.g., accountable executives) present their status updates. Finally, the fifth section is where we review key risks or challenges requiring special attention and discuss noteworthy opportunities. This level and frequency of review and transparency facilitates considerable accountability and collaboration, and at the end of each meeting it's clear whether we're on track to achieve our overall goals and objectives.

Warren Buffet has been quoted as saying, "You never know who's swimming naked until the tide goes out." The business review process holds stakeholders accountable by serving as a metaphorical tide going out—if your area's performance is lagging or you haven't made progress on initiatives, your boss and peers will know about it.

MANAGEMENT GTR ACTION PLAN

Great management is the most effective way to convert ideas and plans into actions and results. A situational assessment to understand the current state will give you the context to determine what needs to be done. Setting priorities both in terms of performance goals and objectives will align stakeholders around a focused set of outcomes. Comprehensive planning will convert goals and objectives into a road map outlining all the action items to achieve success. Organizing for action will help optimize the right team operating model and organizational structure to empower the team to execute. Finally, monitoring implementation with effective management systems will ensure performance and progress are being measured to enable quick and effective adjustments.

Key elements of our Management "Get the Reps" Action Plan are designed to proactively identify opportunities where you can serve as a project manager on a cross-functional project. This will enable you to develop a priority setting and planning process that fits your style and implement a personal self-assessment tool to track wins and setbacks.

MANAGEMENT GTR ACTION PLAN

PLAN

- Undergo a current-state assessment of your management ability to identify your strengths and areas for development
- Devise a comprehensive plan tailored to addressing your areas of development; the development plan should include:
  - A checklist of tasks that you plan to complete to learn, practice, and measure your progress in developing your management ability
  - A list of reading materials, books, and resources that target your areas for development
- Request an opportunity with your company or direct manager to play the role of "project manager" for an upcoming assignment
- Volunteer to join an internal steering committee or cross-collaboration project that requires you to work across teams and potentially play a lead role on one of the workstreams
- Find specific opportunities outside of your current organization that will provide an opportunity to take the lead in managing a project or people on a project

LEARN

- Subscribe to recurring executive coaching webinars, seminars, speaking events, and workshops

- Find an external mentor or business colleague to provide you with mentorship, professional guidance, feedback, and accountability on your development plan
- Ask for feedback from both direct and indirect leaders within your organization regarding your management capabilities; do this on a regularly scheduled cadence
- If you manage employees, ask for feedback on the team's current plan, priorities, and progress and their thoughts around the management systems in place to support it
- If your team does not have a plan, take the opportunity to propose a plan, priorities, and management systems

PRACTICE

- On your next project, develop a fully fleshed-out RACI matrix to help individuals on the project understand their roles, responsibilities, and deliverables
- Put in place or propose that management systems (e.g., Business Reviews) be utilized to monitor progress of priorities
- Practice developing a plan, defining priorities, and establishing goals for your team; work with the team to define tactical action plans
- Propose and implement a team structure and operating model that drive accountability and empower your team to drive action and results
- Develop a professional career cascade for yourself, starting with your personal mission and ending with goals you can set annually

MEASURE

- Observe whether the application of your development is driving actions and results within and across teams; assess the level of engagement with your team and whether the management systems you put in place are effectively holding team members accountable
- Request feedback from mentors, direct and skip-level managers, and peers to provide an assessment of your developing management ability; ask for specific examples to see if their answers match with your intended outcomes

- Track your small "wins" by measuring the number of examples where your management directly empowered others to drive action
- Evaluate your progress and adjust your plan based on feedback so far
- Complete the Management Ability section of the Executive Fundamentals Self-Assessment

CHAPTER 3

LEADERSHIP ABILITY

"The true measure of leadership is influence
—nothing more, nothing less."

—JOHN C. MAXWELL

Leadership is all about delivering results by influencing the thoughts and actions of others. Leaders set the example, they provide forward-looking inspiration, they empower, they encourage, and they motivate their people to find the best way forward to accomplish their objectives.

The best leaders empower groups to work together, to align around common goals and plans to deliver a compelling vision.

They help us see things in different ways and organize our efforts to achieve more than we thought was possible.

> *Great leaders promote inclusion.*

Great leaders promote inclusion. They regularly and consistently involve others in the process of charting a path forward and make the most of the diverse skill sets and experiences that their people bring to each project.

In their book *The Leadership Challenge*, authors James Kouzes and Barry Posner conducted a decade of research with over one thousand leaders and distilled their results into five fundamental practices: Successful leaders model the way, inspire a shared vision, challenge the process, enable others to act, and encourage the heart.

These practices can be learned and put into practice by anyone who wants to become a more effective leader. With these fundamental practices in mind, we can all aspire and improve to become better leaders.

With Kouzes's and Posner's work as a guide, we learn that leadership is a function of five fundamentals:

1. Setting the Example

2. Inspiring an Aligned Vision

3. Empowering Others and Enabling Action

4. Challenging the Status Quo

5. Encouraging and Motivating

SETTING THE EXAMPLE

Kouzes and Posner emphasize the importance of modeling the behavior that you expect of others. "Titles are granted, but it's your behavior that earns you respect." To truly influence the thoughts and actions of others, we have to build and sustain credibility, and there's no better way to do that than to lead by practicing what you preach. To effectively lead by example, first you must be clear on your personal leadership philosophy, because that philosophy outlines your guiding principles. As is clear from its name, a personal leadership philosophy should be personalized and reflect what you truly believe.

As one example, we've outlined our leadership philosophy in the following graphic.

LEADERSHIP PHILOSOPHY

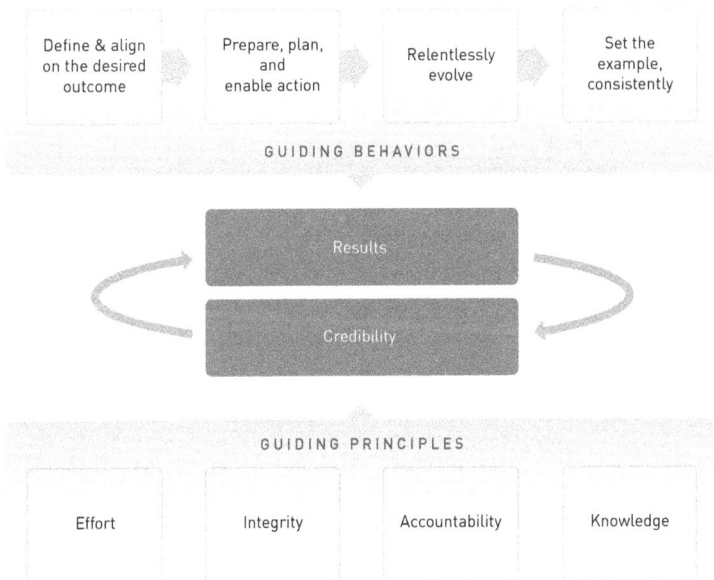

Define & align on the desired outcome	Prepare, plan, and enable action	Relentlessly evolve	Set the example, consistently

GUIDING BEHAVIORS

Results

Credibility

GUIDING PRINCIPLES

Effort	Integrity	Accountability	Knowledge

We like to think of this graphic as representing the "virtuous cycle of results." At the top are the four guiding behaviors we demonstrate consistently in order to deliver results, and across the bottom are the four guiding principles we live by to build and sustain credibility. The more results we deliver, the more credibility we build—which, in turn, opens the door to opportunities to deliver even greater results. This philosophy has evolved over time, and will continue to do so. Sitting on our desks, it serves as a daily reminder about the principles and behaviors we believe in.

A second example is Alan Mulally's "Working Together Principles and Practices."

SKILLED AND MOTIVATED TEAM
WORKING TOGETHER PRINCIPLES AND PRACTICES

- People first
- Everyone is included
- Compelling vision, comprehensive strategy, relentless implementation
- Clear performance goals
- One plan
- Facts and data
- Everyone knows the plan, the status and areas that need special attention
- Propose a plan, "find-a-way" attitude
- Respect, listen, help, and appreciate each other
- Emotional resilience. . . trust the process
- Have fun. . . enjoy the journey and each other

Alan

Although it's a simple list, there's a lot of gold in what Alan believes in. The key takeaway is that a leadership philosophy doesn't have to be a complex framework—it can be simple. Whatever approach you take, it should be personalized, and it should represent how you want to lead.

> *A leadership philosophy doesn't have to be a complex framework—it can be simple.*

Once you've defined your personal leadership philosophy, it's critical that you demonstrate consistency in your behaviors—every day and at all times. The dreaded "say-do" gap (where you don't do what you say you will) is the fastest way to destroy credibility. Building credibility takes great effort over a long period of time, but it can be destroyed in an instant. One of the biggest mistakes I've observed throughout my career is when those in leadership positions assume they don't need to earn and maintain credibility among those they're attempting to lead and focus instead on only building credibility with their superiors. This approach may get your team members to comply, but they'll never be fully engaged. When going into new leadership positions, I've found it helpful to always assume I'm starting with a credibility deficit and that I've got to earn a credibility surplus. Clearly articulating the standards that I hold for myself through a leadership philosophy, and following through by demonstrating consistent behavior has proved to be an effective way to build credibility.

INSPIRING AN ALIGNED VISION

If you want to deliver significant results, everyone must be working together toward a common goal. Although having a compelling vision for the future is key, ensuring it's aligned and shared with stakeholders is of equal, if not more, importance. In his book *Level Three Leadership*, James Clawson outlines the seven levels of "buy-in" to an idea, from lowest to highest: active resistance, passive resistance, apathy, compliance, agreement, engagement, and passion. The level of stakeholder commitment and effort is highly correlated with where they fall on the "buy-in" scale. If you want to maximize buy-in, include stakeholders in the process of defining your vision. Listen to their feedback, and be open-minded about adjusting and evolving your vision so that it becomes a shared vision. It's more work, but in the end, if people feel like they were part of creating an exciting vision, they'll be more engaged and passionate in their efforts to achieve it. In addition, including others' perspectives in the process will help stress-test your ideas and assumptions, almost always resulting in a better outcome.

In one large company I joined, I inherited a sizable team that had experienced frequent leadership turnover; as a result, they were naturally skeptical of the direction in which I was going to lead the team. After getting a good sense of the current state of the team, I got started on aligning the group around a team vision. My approach was simple. The first thing I did was ask all my direct reports to work with their teams individually and then send me their idea of what our team vision should be. We then held an initial offsite with the team managers, and one of the first agenda items we addressed was to look at what everyone had sent to me, side-by-side. I also included my initial idea of our team vision—and remarkably, the ideas all expressed the same concept, but in slightly different ways. After each manager provided the context to what they had sent, we worked together to merge all the visions into a single, unified team vision. Going through the process together helped to get us all aligned, and that alignment showed in how energetic and enthusiastic the managers were when we shared our vision with the broader team.

> *Inspiration energizes and captivates us.*

Because inspiration energizes and captivates us, it is an essential and extraordinarily effective way to increase the level of stakeholder buy-in. In their book *Primal Leadership*, authors Daniel Goleman, Richard Boyatzis, and Annie McKee outline the role inspiration plays in leadership. "Leaders who inspire both create resonance and move people with a compelling vision or a shared mission. Such leaders embody what they ask of others, and are able to articulate a shared mission in a way that inspires others to follow." Putting forth the effort to inspire and align around a shared vision is worth every bit of the time it takes. As Alan Mulally once stated, "One of the most important lessons I've learned throughout my career is the power of a compelling vision."

I had the privilege of witnessing this firsthand early in my career. The CEO at the multi-billion-dollar company I was working for took the time every year to communicate how our vision and strategy had evolved from the prior year and what our annual priorities were going to be for the upcoming year. He didn't simply send out a memo or a prerecorded video—he held an all-day strategy session in an auditorium. And because there were tens of thousands of employees at the time, he held many of these sessions all over the country—it was that important to him. In the three years I had the opportunity to attend the sessions, I remember walking out energized and inspired by what we were trying to accomplish as a company. It became clear why our priorities were what they were, which helped me understand how my role fit within a much bigger picture. I wasn't alone; everyone was inspired and aligned with what our future was all about.

EMPOWERING OTHERS AND ENABLING ACTION

Most of us probably think that being accountable and being responsible for getting things done are the same thing. However, there's an important difference between the two that Scott Eblin concisely describes in his book *The Next Level*. "The difference between responsibility and accountability is the difference between doing and leading." Scott emphasizes the importance of becoming "team-reliant" over "self-reliant" by defining the "what" but letting go of the "how."

> *There's nothing more empowering than having the autonomy to make decisions and pursue outcomes in the way you choose.*

Every year, I go through a process with my direct reports where we cascade our long-term priorities into annual priorities. We do this as a team so we're all aligned around the same set of goals and objectives. From there, each direct report is empowered to work with their teams to develop detailed action plans outlining how they're going to accomplish the goals and objectives they're responsible for. Although I do review the detailed plans and provide perspective when asked, I leave it to the teams to determine the best way to accomplish a particular objective. This has been an effective approach to maintaining accountability while delegating responsibility.

When leaders desire to transition from responsibility to accountability, they must put processes and systems into place that *enable* accountability while ensuring that they do not take on being personally responsible for achieving the organization's desired results.

There's nothing more empowering than having the autonomy to make decisions and pursue outcomes in the way you choose. Delegation of decision rights and responsibility is the single best way to develop others into effective leaders—they learn by doing. When you are early in your career, empowering teams with responsibility while assuming accountability yourself can be uncomfortable: Your success now depends on the ability of your teams to deliver results. This is why structuring the management systems and practices (such as those outlined in the management chapter under "Monitoring Implementation") to enable effective accountability are so important. Effective management systems allow leaders to pivot to where their help is needed so they can provide support and remove obstacles. As Ronald Heifetz and Donald Laurie say in "The Work of Leadership," "Letting people take the initiative in defining and solving problems means that management needs to learn to support rather than control."[1]

---

1   Ronald Heifetz and Donald Laurie, "The Work of Leadership," *Harvard Business Review* (January–February 1997), p. 129.

CHALLENGING THE STATUS QUO

We are all aware that managing change is a core component of effective leadership. As Ronald Heifetz and Donald Laurie put it in their article "The Work of Leadership," "Instead of maintaining norms, leaders have to challenge the 'way we do business.'" There's always a better way to do something, and finding that way is a function of adopting the mindset to relentlessly evolve and innovate—to keep putting points on the board to deliver small wins. Alan Mulally lived his principle to "always be working on a better plan" during his turnaround efforts at both Boeing and Ford. Jim Clawson believes that "leadership without the ability to manage change is powerless," and defines leaders' "change quotient" by their ability to recognize the need for change, become emotionally comfortable with change, and finally, to master the change process.

■ ■ ■

The greatest opportunities to add value to the organization are when significant change is needed. In my first role leading a department, I had no idea I was walking into a situation that was going to require a complete transformation. Within the first few months, I discovered the considerable challenges that needed to be addressed. The employees on the team were not very engaged, and morale was suffering. As a functional department, we were no longer creating value for internal customers. We were operating inefficiently and ineffectively, and progress was nearly at a standstill. I quickly came to the realization that I was likely never going to walk into a leadership situation where some level of change was not needed, and I decided to leverage this opportunity to start developing a change process that I could adapt to fit my leadership and management style.

In their book *Leading Successful Change*, authors Gregory Shea and Cassie Solomon frame the change process in their "Work Systems

Model." They state that organizational change requires transforming the behavior of thousands or even tens of thousands of people, and to do so effectively requires changing their work environment. They believe that a successful change initiative requires using at least four of their eight levers of change:

1. Organization
2. Workplace design
3. Task
4. People
5. Rewards
6. Measurement
7. Information distribution
8. Decision allocation

During our departmental turnaround, our focus areas were organization, people, measurement, and workplace design. Because we were a functional department with internal customers, we put in the time to understand how we could add the most value to the business, and we restructured our organization to match these needs. In doing so, we uncovered the need to close several capability gaps among our existing staff. This required us to recruit the right people for certain roles, and in some cases this meant that existing staff members were no longer the right fit. With the right roles and people, we established a measurement framework where goals, objectives, and responsibilities were clear and transparent and aligned with internal customer outcomes. Finally, we discovered that sitting in a different building from our primary business partners was not the most effective structure, so we changed our workplace design so that we were all in the same location.

■ ■ ■

In his book *Leading Change*, John Kotter identifies two patterns from studying successful change initiatives: "First, useful change tends to be associated with a multistep process that creates power and motivation sufficient to overwhelm all the sources of inertia. Second, the process is never employed effectively unless it is driven by high-quality leadership, not just excellent management."

KOTTER'S EIGHT-STAGE PROCESS OF CREATING MAJOR CHANGE

1- Establishing a sense of urgency

2- Creating the guiding coalition

3- Developing a vision and strategy

4- Communicating the change vision

5- Empowering broad-based action

6- Generating short-term wins

7- Consolidating gains and producing more change

8- Anchoring new approaches in the culture

If we aren't growing, we're dying. To stay in a perpetual state of progress, we've found it helpful to do two things. First, adopt a mindset of "relentless evolution." Whether the focus is as an individual or an organizational leader, small wins and evolutions over long periods make a big difference. Second, develop a change management competency that can serve as an adaptable playbook when change is needed. We've found significant value from the frameworks in

Leading Change and *Leading Successful Change*, but there are many other effective examples to learn from.

ENCOURAGING AND MOTIVATING

"Recognition is the most powerful currency you have, and it costs you nothing," says Jessica Herrin in the book *The Leadership Challenge* by James Kouzes and Barry Posner. And John Kotter articulates concisely in *What Leaders Really Do*, "Motivation and inspiration energize people, not by pushing them in the right direction as control mechanisms do but by satisfying basic human needs for achievement."

Consistent and regular recognition—however small—goes a long way toward building a high level of morale and engagement. And we're not talking about big awards that must happen on a public stage. The more consistent, "Thank you. You did a fantastic job!" bits of recognition can often have the greatest impact. People want to feel that what they do is of value and that their work is noticed and appreciated. When I started leading larger teams, I made it a point to regularly discuss with my managers the great work the team was doing. Afterward, I'd stop by the desk of the individuals to say thank you and let them know they were doing a great job. Although the team members certainly appreciated the public recognition for earning our team awards in our monthly all-hands meetings, I received consistent feedback in our team engagement surveys that what they appreciated most was the company leaders personally showing appreciation for their work.

In their book *Why Should Anyone Be Led by You?*, authors Rob Goffee and Gareth Jones state, "Inspirational leaders empathize passionately—and realistically—with people, and they care intensely about the work employees do." Early in my career, I had the opportunity to lead an important presentation where the audience was a group of senior executives. I was working within a culture where it was common and accepted for attendees to be multitasking on their laptops during meetings. When the most senior executive arrived at this particular meeting, he did not bring his laptop with him. He had only a printed copy of the presentation. From the moment he sat down, he was 100 percent present despite the fact that the presenter (myself) was six promotions junior to him. He treated me as though I were an equal in the room, which had a profound effect on how I viewed the importance of not only what I was presenting, but the role I played in the company. I walked out of the meeting with a strong desire to deliver my absolute best.

Creating motivation in the face of adversity is also a critical component to effective leadership. It's easy to look great as a leader when everything is working well and no significant obstacles are present. But when everything suddenly stops working and times truly turn tough, that's when real leadership is so strongly needed and so clearly revealed. Being an effective leader means finding ways to relate to people, understanding how they're feeling, finding out what drives them, and empathizing with what scares them. These are the all-important steps you must take if you want to influence the thoughts and actions of others during challenging times.

LEADERSHIP GTR ACTION PLAN

Great leadership opens the door to harnessing the power of the collective to achieve extraordinary results. When you set a strong example, you provide a clear pathway to follow. An inspiring and aligned vision brings everyone together in the pursuit of a common destination, and by delegating responsibility and clearing obstacles, you empower people and enable action to take place. If you maintain a relentless focus on finding a better way, you will keep your group on the leading edge of progress.

. . .

Finally, it's essential that you provide regular encouragement and motivation, especially when times get tough, as that will keep everyone moving—no matter the challenges. The key elements of our Leadership "Get the Reps" Action Plan are the following: identifying mentors who exhibit exemplary leadership, acquiring more knowledge through a customized reading plan, and developing your own leadership philosophy to set your own standard of how you want to lead.

LEADERSHIP GTR ACTION PLAN

PLAN

- Undergo a current-state assessment of your leadership ability to identify your strengths and areas for development
- Devise a comprehensive plan tailored to addressing your areas of development; the development plan should include:
  - A checklist of tasks that you plan to complete within a specific period of time to learn, practice, and measure your progress in developing your leadership ability
  - A list of reading materials, books, and resources that target your areas for development
  - The creation of your individualized leadership philosophy and values
- Apply for any internal programs that provide opportunities to exemplify your leadership abilities
- Discuss your career-path options with your direct manager to identify ways to increase your scope over time

LEARN

- Study past leaders across different verticals to understand their perspectives on leadership
- Take the example of leaders within your organization who have exemplary fundamentals
- Build a relationship with 1–2 internal executives who can provide mentorship
- Request frequent feedback from both direct and indirect leaders within your organization regarding your leadership capabilities

PRACTICE

- Work with your team (no matter the size) to develop a shared vision and purpose that everyone can work toward
- Look to mobilize a project team to help a pressing business or team challenge
- Find opportunities to directly thank or show appreciation for work done for you
- Take a project that is currently underperforming and find a potentially new solution and map out a better plan that would help turn around performance
- Identify your top four guiding behaviors and principles; start with small opportunities to build up to bigger ones
- Take the time to respect, listen, and help other members of your team

MEASURE

- Observe whether the application of your development is driving actions and results within and across your team
- Request feedback from mentors, direct and skip-level managers, and peers to provide an assessment of your developing management ability; ask for specific examples to see if their answers match with your intended outcomes.

- Track your small "wins" by measuring the number of times your recognition of others and your leadership brought individuals together to deliver results
- Evaluate your progress and adjust your plan based on feedback so far
- Complete the Leadership Ability section of the Executive Fundamentals Self-Assessment

CHAPTER 4

EXECUTIVE INTELLIGENCE

"Credibility is a leader's currency. With it, he or she
is solvent; without it, he or she is bankrupt."

—JOHN C. MAXWELL

Executive intelligence is about catalyzing and sustaining credibility. Whether you're trying to convince someone on your team to follow you or trying to influence a stakeholder to accept your advice, your credibility with those individuals determines how they'll respond. Well-developed executive intelligence increases the pace at which credibility is established and enables credibility to be sustained over the long term.

We like to define executive intelligence as the intersection of emotional intelligence and executive presence. Emotional intelligence and executive presence greatly impact how others perceive you, often unconsciously. It's this perception that affects how much credibility you're given—which ultimately determines how much influence you'll have.

Daniel Goleman, in his essay "What Makes a Leader?",[1] states that emotional intelligence requires self-awareness and control, as well as social awareness and understanding. As humans, we are drawn to individuals who possess self-confidence and who are consistently adaptable and resilient. We are particularly drawn to people who listen as well as they communicate, who are empathetic, who are invested in developing others, and who effectively manage and resolve conflict. All of these qualities come into play in emotional intelligence and can make or break an aspiring leader.

Developing effective emotional intelligence takes time and can be difficult, but it's well worth the effort. In their book *Switch: How to Change Things When Change Is Hard*, authors Chip Heath and Dan Heath elegantly illustrate why, and we can learn valuable information from their work. They compare the brain's two independent systems to a rider and an elephant. The rider represents the rational side of the brain, whereas the elephant represents the emotional side. Under normal circumstances, the rider is in control of the elephant. But the instant the elephant gets spooked and goes wild, the rider is helpless. The analogy is effective, because we can probably all relate to moments when our emotions caused a reaction we wish had never happened—or to use the Heaths' analogy, our rider lost control of our elephant. The difficulty in developing emotional intelligence is not only in developing more control of our own emotions, but also in understanding how to appeal to both the rational and emotional side of others to influence them to act.

1   Daniel Goleman, "What Makes a Leader?" *Harvard Business Review* (January 2004).

> *Well-developed executive intelligence is exceptional, and it is nearly instantly recognizable.*

When we speak of executive presence, we are really talking about executive gravitas and communication. We define executive gravitas as your observable presence. It's how you act, how you behave, and how you look. It's about having confidence and consistency under fire and about displaying decisive decision-making. It means balancing approachability with seriousness while maintaining polished body language. We think of executive communication as your audible presence. It's how you speak and how you articulate your thoughts. Well-developed executive intelligence is exceptional, and it is nearly instantly recognizable. It creates an immediate credibility surplus that accomplished leaders need to influence stakeholders. Executive intelligence is a function of five fundamentals.

EXECUTIVE INTELLIGENCE FUNDAMENTALS

1. Emotional Awareness
2. Emotional Management
3. Executive Gravitas
4. Executive Communication
5. Development Awareness

EMOTIONAL AWARENESS

We define emotional awareness as understanding how situations will affect both your emotions and others' emotions. What we define as emotional awareness, Travis Bradberry and Jean Greaves define as *self-awareness* and *social-awareness* in their book, *Emotional Intelligence 2.0.*

When you have developed a keen sense of self-awareness, you understand how different situations will affect you, you know what motivates you, and you know what gets your emotions elevated. When you have a strong sense of what your values are, you will have a strong sense of self-confidence when you're in your element.

Bradberry and Greaves say, "Self-awareness is not about discovering deep, dark secrets or unconscious motivations, but, rather, it comes from developing a straightforward and honest understanding of what makes you tick." This is important, because developing awareness will improve your ability to navigate difficult situations.

Let's focus on a key element of self-awareness: understanding the drivers of the various emotional reactions that we can have to specific events. If, over time, we put in the effort to understand ourselves by reflecting on our own actions and emotions, we can pinpoint the causes of these emotional responses and their results. This ability is extraordinarily useful, because it allows us to prepare for how our emotions might be affected before we enter into important situations.

To use an example, imagine you are about to walk onto a stage to give a keynote speech in front of five hundred people. Many of us would be feeling anxious and nervous as the adrenaline surges into our system. Almost everyone knows how they'd feel walking unprepared onto that stage. So, most of us prepare—we write out our speech, and then we practice it over and over again until we feel comfortable we've got it down. If we can anticipate the potential emotional effects of all the important situations we might face, we can prepare for them as we would before giving a keynote speech. Doing this preparation lays the groundwork for getting to a point where we can better control our emotional reactions in any given scenario—which is a crucial skill for any leader.

Bradberry and Greaves define social awareness as "the ability to accurately pick up on emotions in other people and understand what is really going on with them." A critical component to any leader's social awareness is found in the ability to be empathetic—that is, the ability to understand how the current situation, environment, or what you're about to say will impact another person's emotions. Empathy serves as a great "social sensor," enabling you to understand the feelings in the room. Social awareness can also encompass an individual's ability to quickly sense and understand the social networks and political dynamics of a specific group. Honing your ability to understand what's behind the behaviors of others and anticipating how their behaviors may change is a major step in improving control of your own emotions and, subsequently, effectively managing the relationships of those around you.

EMOTIONAL MANAGEMENT

We define emotional management as your ability to both control your own emotions and navigate through situations with others in a way that harnesses the constructive power of emotions. What we define as emotional management, Bradberry and Greaves define as *self-management* and *relationship management*. Self-management, they say, is your ability to manage how your own emotions affect your behavior. However, it's more than just the ability to control impulses and maintain self-control when your emotions are under attack, although that's a big part of it. The following abilities, based on those described in *Primal Leadership*, are also key elements of maintaining effective emotional self-management:

1. The ability to stay flexible and motivated during times of change
2. The ability to maintain optimism and a level of resilience no matter what is thrown your way
3. The ability to take the initiative and put forth the relentless effort in pursuit of achievement
4. The ability to hold yourself accountable and maintain high levels of discipline, integrity, and authenticity at all times

Some leaders are lucky enough to have many, if not all, of these traits as innate characteristics. But most of us have to work at developing these traits where they're weak, and the way to do this is through discipline. Once we acknowledge our weaknesses, we can get to work changing those weaknesses into effective habits that we no longer have to think twice about. It's helpful to start by improving control of your own emotions in a single situation where you have awareness of how the situation is going to affect how you feel.

For example, let's say you get irritated quickly when driving in heavy traffic and habitually tell others what you think about their driving skills despite the fact they can't hear you. If you can anticipate this is going to happen and draw on your experience as to how it's going to make you feel, you can work on not reacting negatively in those kinds of situations. You're still going to feel the same emotional response, and your goal is not to stop that from happening— your goal is to build the discipline to not let that feeling affect your behavior. It will be difficult at first, but eventually you'll be able to override the feeling and not respond—without even thinking about it. You can take this same approach and apply it from situation to situation, eventually getting to a point to where you've dramatically improved your ability to control your emotions.

Bradberry and Greaves tell us that relationship management is your ability to understand others' emotions in order to manage interactions successfully. It's extraordinarily effective to leverage an emotional connection when you are trying to influence the thoughts and actions of others because being "moved" to action is more powerful than being "reasoned" to action. In other words, the best effort is brought out in people when they want to do something vs. doing something simply because they think they should. For example, contrast someone who is passionate about the work they do with someone who doesn't like their work but needs a paycheck. Logically, they both need to work to earn money and pay bills, but there would almost certainly be a big disparity in each one's level of commitment and effort.

Although it might be impossible to get the second person to become passionate about their work, finding a way to link the work to a greater and more meaningful purpose comes from a connection on a more emotional level and is likely to improve their overall engagement.

We think it's useful to point out some key elements in maintaining effective relationship management—again, these are based on elements from *Primal Leadership*:

1. The ability to inspire and influence others
2. The ability to foster teamwork and collaboration with a commitment to developing others
3. The ability to negotiate and manage through conflict
4. The ability to effectively communicate

While discipline is the primary ingredient in improving self-management deficiencies, practice is the primary ingredient for relationship management. We all have varying degrees of potential with respect to how developed our self-management or relationship-management skills can become. In other words, some people are born with an innate ability to better control their emotional reactions and empathize with others, while others have short fuses and can be almost oblivious to what's going on around them. That said, everyone can improve their baseline—and the goal for each of us is to maximize our individual potential.

Reaching that goal comes from practice—in other words, doing the repetitions that are required for us to be good at whatever we are trying to perfect. Learning to better manage our own emotional reactions will provide insight into how varying situations will affect others. It's also important to develop the habit of thinking through how our own decisions, behaviors, and actions will impact the emotional reactions of others. At first, there may be a big difference between the actual reactions of others vs. how you thought they would react. Over time, however, thinking through your actions will improve your ability to predict the most likely responses, allowing you to adjust your approach beforehand and improve the outcomes.

EXECUTIVE GRAVITAS

In *Executive Presence*, Sylvia Hewlett defines gravitas as "how you act." We extend this definition to include all aspects of your observable presence—both how you act and how you look. Regarding how you act, gravitas starts with a high level of confidence and your ability to stay composed under intense, highly stressful situations. It means you're able to keep pushing forward, you know how to navigate through tough circumstances, and that you hold steady in your decision-making, no matter what's going on around you.

At the battle of Gettysburg during the American Civil War, General Robert E. Lee, commander of the Confederate forces, led a massive frontal assault on the final day of the battle known as Pickett's Charge. General Winfield Hancock commanded the Union defenses and was actively involved in directing his troops. When he was told that he was risking his life by riding on horseback after the battle was in full swing, his response was said to have been, "There are times when a corps commander's life does not count." Hancock continued leading his troops until he was wounded in action—that's gravitas. The takeaway from this example is that gravitas has a big impact on all who observe you. Particularly in very tough situations, exceptional gravitas can inspire, build confidence, and unify a group of people.

The ability to balance approachability with temperance and seriousness is also a key factor in how your gravitas is perceived. In her book *All the Leader You Can Be*, Suzanne Bates breaks executive presence into three groups—character, substance, and style. She also defines a key element of character as "restraint," which she defines as moderation and reasonableness. From what we've observed, restraint has been one of the most essential behaviors in those people who have well-developed gravitas. When you decide to use humor selectively, or you pause and think before responding to a question or a challenge, or you master control of your emotions, you are exhibiting important elements of a well-developed gravitas.

Finally, we have to stress the importance of body language. Sitting and standing straight, making eye contact, projecting high levels of energy, and limiting overly animated gestures all make a difference. Similarly, people do judge you and draw initial impressions based on how you look. It's important to fit within the social norms of the environment where you work, but it's equally important that within those norms, you're polished and dressed well.

For example, I remember one high-potential manager with aspirations to be promoted to a director. As part of his annual performance review, he received 360-degree feedback from several cross-functional stakeholders. They stated that although he was considered to be an exceptional manager, it was difficult for them to envision him as a director. When he asked for my advice, I recommended that he start by considering the initial impression he was making when he met stakeholders for the first time. We started with his appearance: He usually wore jeans and a polo, and he always walked into meetings with a backpack on. These practices were completely normal and acceptable for managers and technical analysts within the organization, but directors generally dressed in more professional business attire. As a result, anyone meeting him for the first time unconsciously assumed he was more junior than a director—solely based on his appearance. It may be unfortunate, but once an initial impression is made, it's difficult to change that perception. Although by no means a guarantee for a promotion, if he had been dressing like the other directors, it would have been easier for stakeholders to envision him as one during promotion discussions.

EXECUTIVE COMMUNICATION

Your audible presence—how you speak and articulate your thoughts—is also an important factor in the way you are perceived. A leader who speaks well and can captivate an audience generally has a mastery of vocabulary, proper grammar, tone, cadence, and the appropriate use of filler words. Some elements of our audible presence such as our voice depth are out of our control. But, let's take a look at areas where we can work on developing and improving executive communication.

VOCABULARY

The ultimate purpose of any communication is for the listener to fully understand the message of the speaker. A successful communicator will strike the right balance. If you use vocabulary that is too advanced, esoteric, or jargon-laden, your audience will lose the meaning of your words, and you will automatically inhibit your ability to reach them. On the other hand, using vocabulary that is beneath your audience can negatively affect their perception of you and your authority to speak on your topic. A leader's goal should be to build a robust vocabulary so that the efficiency and effectiveness of your communication will be enhanced, and your audience will appreciate and act upon your intended message. One of the best ways to build vocabulary is to read on a regular basis and take the time to understand the definitions of unfamiliar words. Sometimes the simplest and most obvious practices are the most effective.

CADENCE

Many people speak quickly, particularly when they're nervous. Besides being more difficult to understand, the message from a fast-talker may often create the impression that they have limited control of their topic as well as a lack of refinement. To make your message the best it can be, it's useful to practice a more paced cadence that will allow for more effective modulation and tone consistency.

FILLER WORDS

The heavy use of filler words can make listening to any leader's message like listening to a jackhammer. Words like *um*, *ah*, *you know*, *sort of*, and *right* do not help with effective message delivery. The simplest way to avoid using these words is to become comfortable with pauses. It may feel strange at first, because we're generally uncomfortable with silence. However, replacing filler words with pauses will greatly enhance the refinement of your communication and is much more pleasant for the listener.

The key to great communication is practice and preparation. There is no substitute. Every aspiring leader will want to take the time to get it right.

DEVELOPMENT AWARENESS

I've had the privilege to work with many extraordinarily high-potential individuals throughout my career. One of the most consistent characteristics of this exceptional cohort of people is they all have a relentless desire to be better. When they receive development feedback, they immediately get to work to improve. When it comes to career success, we believe the true "X-factor" is development awareness, which is the ability to accurately self-assess fundamental weaknesses and self-correct, leading to what we call executive intuition. We'll revisit this idea in more detail in the next chapter, but, for now, think of executive intuition as the ability to convert new knowledge into unconscious pattern-recognition. It's the ability to instinctively and immediately draw from your entire base of knowledge and experience without thinking about it. In other words, it's your mental muscle-memory. The greater your development awareness, the more unconscious competency you're able to build. Executive development is a career-long journey, and it's those with an insatiable desire to continuously develop and improve who will evolve into the most exemplary executives.

It's helpful to think of each individual fundamental skill in terms of a scale from 0 to 100, with 100 representing the maximum attainable skill level by the most gifted human being. Each of us has a personal baseline somewhere above, but close to, the bottom. The difference between 0 and our personal baseline is our "natural talent," which is what we're born with. This is different for each individual and each of their fundamental skills. Somewhere above the personal baseline is our "current skill level," with the distance between them representing what you've developed to date. This development is a culmination of all your knowledge, experiences, and development efforts. Somewhere above the "current skill level" but more than likely below the top is your "personal max potential." Like the personal baseline, this is different for each skill and individual. The distance between your current skill level and your max potential is your "development opportunity."

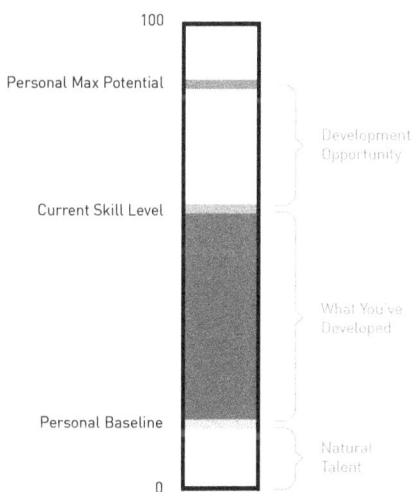

To illustrate what we mean, we'll take two somewhat extreme examples. We'll call the first example Tara Talent. Tara Talent has considerable natural talent, but she is also completely unaware that she has innate talent and hasn't put forth any effort to develop her

TARA TALENT

Business Acumen | **Management Ability** | **Leadership Ability** | **Executive Intelligence**

Current Skill Level

Current Skill Level

Current Skill Level

Current Skill Level

Natural Talent

Natural Talent

Natural Talent

Natural Talent

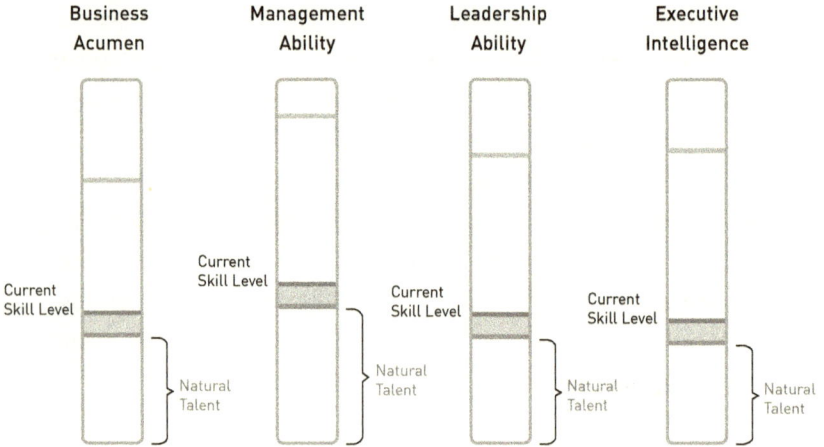

ELAINE EFFORT

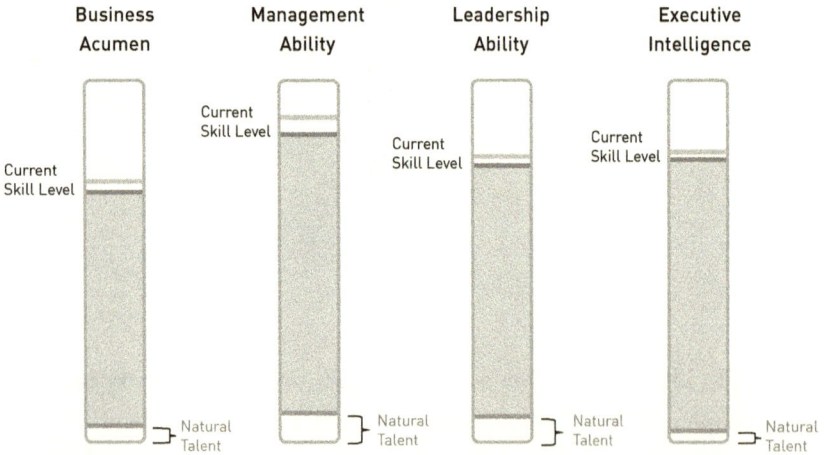

Business Acumen | **Management Ability** | **Leadership Ability** | **Executive Intelligence**

Current Skill Level

Current Skill Level

Current Skill Level

Current Skill Level

Natural Talent

Natural Talent

Natural Talent

Natural Talent

abilities. As a result, Tara Talent's current skill level is hovering modestly above her natural talent level.

We'll call the second example Elaine Effort. Elaine Effort has far less natural talent than Tara Talent, but she has spent her entire career focused on her own development. As a result, Elaine's current skill level is close to her max potential and far higher than Tara's, despite the fact that she started from a much lower baseline. The takeaway? *Effort is the only thing that can top talent.*

It's difficult to know exactly where your max potential is across each fundamental skill, but that's not what's important. The key to development awareness is a realistic assessment of your current skill level and the relentless desire and pursuit of getting as close to your personal max potential as possible. And because you'll never know if you've reached your max potential, you must adopt the mindset of continuous, career-long development.

EXECUTIVE INTELLIGENCE GTR ACTION PLAN

Well-developed executive intelligence is the foundation upon which credibility is built. With emotional awareness, we can go into situations understanding the emotional reactions not only of ourselves, but also of others who are involved. Emotional management then gives us the ability to control how we respond to our emotions and empathize with those around us. Developing executive gravitas and communication will improve our ability to catalyze credibility, as our level of influence increases with improved visual and audible presence.

Finally, development awareness reminds us that we can always improve and get better at what we do. Key elements of our Executive Intelligence "Get the Reps" Action Plan are to obtain feedback on a regular basis, create opportunities to present and speak to larger groups, and become comfortable with uncomfortable situations by finding challenging opportunities to build your emotional resilience.

EXECUTIVE INTELLIGENCE
GTR ACTION PLAN

PLAN

- Undergo a current-state assessment of your executive intelligence to identify your strengths and areas for development
- Devise a comprehensive plan tailored to addressing your areas of development; the development plan should include:
  - A checklist of tasks that you plan to complete to learn, practice, and measure your progress in developing your executive intelligence
  - A list of reading materials, books, and resources that target your areas for development
- Discuss with your manager opportunities to join or listen in on executive-level meetings or strategy discussions
- Proactively find ways to present and deliver your work to executive teams
- Identify opportunities for public speaking and engagements that allow you to present your work
- Prepare in advance for challenging conversations and meetings that will test your emotional composure

LEARN

- Identify leaders in your organization who can provide feedback on their impression of your overall presence and influence during meetings

- Build a relationship with 1–2 key internal executives who you can look to for mentorship and guidance
- Observe the exemplary behaviors (communication, style, conduct, gravitas) of leaders within your organization and take note of how they act on those behaviors

PRACTICE

- Take every form of communication as an opportunity to showcase your executive intelligence (i.e., emails, touch bases, formal presentations, working sessions, etc.)
- Make your speech clear, concise, and consistent with as few filler words as possible in both written and oral form
- Become comfortable in uncomfortable situations by taking on challenging projects
- Dress for success!
- Stay positive and take a moment each week to consciously reflect on your wins and your journey thus far

MEASURE

- Reflect on your level of composure during challenging discussions to understand the types of conversations that may trigger your emotional state
- Provide yourself with an honest assessment of your effort in developing your executive intelligence
- Track your small "wins" by measuring the number of individuals you were able to influence with ideas you communicated
- Evaluate your progress and adjust your plan based on feedback so far
- Complete the Executive Intelligence section of the Executive Fundamentals Self-Assessment

DOING WHAT

PART II

YOU KNOW

CHAPTER 5

EXECUTIVE DEVELOPMENT

"Intelligence, imagination, and knowledge are essential resources,
but only effectiveness converts them into results."

—PETER DRUCKER

I was fortunate that my first real corporate role was in investor relations. The nature of the role afforded quite a bit of face time with a public company CFO, which was quite unusual for someone as junior as I was. I distinctly remember one conversation where he provided some simple advice. He said that he required all the executives who reported to him to read Marshall Goldsmith's book, *What Got You Here Won't Get You There*. His point was simple: The playbook for achieving career success changes with increasing levels of responsibility—and if you don't evolve the skills in your playbook, you'll struggle to continue achieving success.

I didn't fully understand the importance of his advice at the time, but I never forgot what he said. Looking back today, it's clear that professional development is a career-long journey. A journey that constantly requires existing skills to be improved and new skills to be developed. To help articulate our approach to executive development, we've divided this chapter into four sections.

First, we'll build upon the concept of executive intuition and show how it complements the executive point of view and how you go about developing it.

Second, we'll introduce an approach built around what we consider the five key career transition points or levels. We'll show how to approach each level with the mindset of a CEO and how this approach catalyzes your own behaviors and habits so they can be scaled at each point.

Third, we'll transition to our executive development plans, which we believe are not only part of an effective framework but are fully aligned with our goal of developing scalable behaviors and habits.

Finally, we'll outline a framework for execution and monitoring of development progress.

DEVELOPING EXECUTIVE INTUITION

As we said at the beginning of the book, any skill we've acquired requires first knowing what to do and then doing the thousands or even tens of thousands of repetitions required for the skill to become engrained. The golf swing is a perfect example, because it requires knowing the right mechanics and then executing those mechanics flawlessly on every swing. A properly executed grip, stance, back-swing, and downswing all need to come together for us to hit the ball well. The same goes for developing executive intuition.

Noel Burch of Gordon Training International developed a theory that describes the four stages of competency we all go through when learning any new skill:

- *Unconscious incompetence*: your unawareness that you aren't skilled at something. Continuing with the golf swing example, imagine yourself walking onto the driving range for the first time with absolutely no direction. You've never held a club before and are completely on your own. Before your first swing, you would simply not know how good or bad you were, given your lack of prior experience.

- *Conscious incompetence*: your awareness that you aren't skilled at something. After those first several swings, you'd start to learn your skill level. This is the most humbling stage, because it is when you first become aware of how good or bad you are, before you have put forth any effort to improve. In other words, you have no idea how to grip the club, what your stance should be, how to execute a backswing, etc.

- *Conscious competence*: your demonstration of skill at something solely through a focused effort. If, after becoming aware of your lack of skill, you learned how to grip, stand, backswing, down-swing, etc., and then followed through with a lot of practice, you'd get to conscious competence. At this stage, you still must focus on getting the grip right and how you're standing and swinging, but you can execute when concentrating. As soon as you stop focusing, everything falls apart.

- *Unconscious competence*: You demonstrate skill at something instinctively, without having to think about it. At this point on the golf course, you've put forth so much effort that how to grip, position your stance, and swing has become muscle memory. You no longer have to focus or concentrate to execute competently; it simply happens.

We don't often think of walking as a skill, but it is something we all had to learn how to do. When was the last time you thought about the mechanics of walking? This is a simple example of a skill that for most people has become an unconscious competence. You no longer have to think about it: You just get up and walk. With regards to developing executive fundamentals, the idea and goal is the same: to identify fundamental skills where you don't have a great level of competence and do the work so the skill becomes as close to second nature as possible.

In his book *Thinking, Fast and Slow*, Daniel Kahneman outlines two systems that describe thinking. The first system (thinking fast) uses your automatic mental processing that happens without thought. For example, your ability to drive your car while having an in-depth conversation on the phone is an example of your first system at work. We would argue that your fast thinking ability is a function of the skills that have become part of your unconscious competence. The second system (thinking slow) comes into play when you're consciously focusing on specific details to form thoughts. An example would be plotting a four hundred–mile road trip in a way that avoids traffic.

This framework is helpful for contextualizing how we think about executive intuition and executive point of view. Everything you've learned and experienced—from foundational business concepts to how industries work to people management to leadership challenges—ends up in what we call your "experiences and knowledge reservoir," or EKR for short. Business acumen—our first fundamental outlined in chapter one—comprises a significant portion of your EKR and is what you draw from to form an effective executive point of view. In simple terms, *it's your basis for conscious decision-making*. We think this most aligns with Kahneman's description of your slow thinking, system two.

On the other hand, we call the muscle memory equivalent of a skilled executive leader their "executive intuition." Executive intuition is instinctively and simultaneously navigating, managing, and leading in different situations without hesitation. In simple terms, *it's your basis for subconscious decision-making*. We think this most aligns with Kahneman's description of your fast thinking, system one.

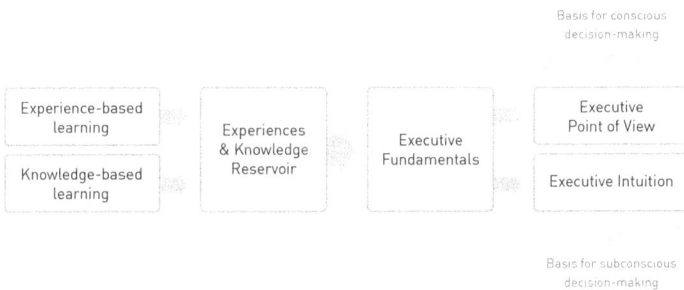

Basis for conscious
decision-making

Experience-based learning				Executive Point of View
	Experiences & Knowledge Reservoir	Executive Fundamentals		
Knowledge-based learning				Executive Intuition

Basis for subconscious
decision-making

To illustrate how executive point of view and executive intuition work together, consider the following: The quality of the outcomes an executive is responsible for delivering is a function of every decision made. "Reasoned decisions" are decisions like which strategy to pursue, how to respond to a recessionary environment, etc. These decisions are made consciously, are thought through, and are not only driven by your EPV but the EPV of everyone included in the decision-making process. "Automatic decisions" are decisions like your immediate response to a colleague asking your advice to a business problem they're dealing with, how you respond to a direct report who just told you they didn't complete an action item they were responsible for, etc. These decisions are made subconsciously and are not consciously thought through, driven by your executive intuition.

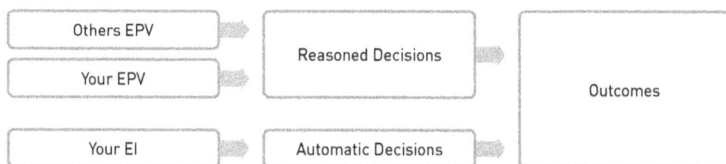

Others EPV	Reasoned Decisions	Outcomes
Your EPV		
Your EI	Automatic Decisions	

Generally speaking, the difference between "reasoned" and "automatic" decisions is that the former are fewer in quantity with each individual decision of greater significance in terms of the final outcomes. The latter are far greater in quantity but with each individual decision of lesser significance. Furthermore, when it comes to subconscious, automatic decisions, the benefit of others' executive intuition is not relevant the way it is with reasoned decision and EPV. For example, if you're the CEO of a company that recently acquired a business in a market you have no experience in, you can surround yourself with people that do have experience, so their EPVs can make up for your EPV shortfalls. However, because your automatic decisions happen subconsciously, you're on your own. This emphasizes the importance of developing executive intuition that results in high-quality automatic decision-making.

The most effective way to develop your executive intuition is to grow your EKR and develop new fundamental skills to the point of unconscious competence. For example, when I first became a manager, I remember reading as much on the topic as I could, eventually acknowledging that, up until that point, my management skills had been an unconscious incompetence. Eventually, that learning, applied with trying, failing, and adjusting, led to the management framework in this book. I used this framework as a checklist for every role and project I was responsible for thereafter.

Eventually, I no longer needed the checklist, and the management framework became second nature. This evolution took place over several years, with many repetitions. The simple part is having the development awareness to constantly seek skills where there's a need for development. The hard part is doing the work, putting in the repetitions required to convert "lack of skill" to a skill that's second nature.

Executive intuition is a function of developing knowledge and skills to a point where you no longer have to think about it; you simply act. Being aware of what to focus on and following through by putting forth the effort to move a particular skill into your subconscious is not a one-time event; as we've said before, it's a career-long journey.

CAREER TRANSITIONS WITH A CEO MINDSET

If you're pursuing a career in business, you likely aspire to be promoted to the executive ranks. Many people who are extraordinarily successful early on, with promotions coming easily, get frustratingly stuck after a few years. Getting stuck is often a result of assuming what made you successful thus far will make you successful going forward. What we often don't think about are the key transition points that require deliberate evolution relative to the way you approach your role. We believe there are five key career points or levels that require you to evolve and work differently. At each level, there's a step change in accountability, which requires a different skill set in order for you to be successful.

FIVE TRANSITIONARY CAREER LEVELS

Level 1
Individual Contributor—where you're responsible for yourself and your work

Level 2
Manager—where you're accountable for individual contributors and their work

Level 3
Director—where you're accountable for managers and their work

Level 4
Functional Executive—where you're accountable for the results of a subfunction or department

Level 5
Enterprise Executive—where you're a member of the enterprise executive team and responsible for the results of an entire enterprise, business unit, or function

As an individual contributor (Level 1), you're responsible for your own deliverables. You can directly control the quality of your results based on the effort you're willing to invest. Smart, driven individuals have no trouble excelling at Level 1, particularly if they have demonstrated strong business acumen—the first fundamental.

Transitioning to Level 2 is the first experience an aspiring leader has in moving from being *responsible* to being *accountable*. In other words, as a manager, you're now accountable for the results that other individual contributors are responsible for delivering. As a manager, developing management ability—the second fundamental—will be critical to succeeding.

Level 3 is where leadership ability—the third fundamental—starts to become especially important. At this level, you're now leading a team where your direct reports have direct reports. Your job becomes creating a high-performance culture that empowers a group to work together and align around common goals to deliver meaningful outcomes. Level 3 is where you fully transition to team reliance and where you define and align what needs to be done, while empowering the team to determine how to do it.

At Level 4, as a member of a functional leadership team, your focus evolves to positioning your team to manage key functional projects and initiatives. You need to not only effectively *lead* your area of responsibility, but you also need to emerge as a functional leader who works together with other executives to deliver on functional priorities. The fourth fundamental—executive intelligence— becomes especially important at Level 4 because you must have credibility and influence to succeed as a functional leader.

At Level 5, you're one of the most senior executives within the organization and a member of the enterprise executive team. The scope of your role and responsibilities is large enough that your focus evolves to positioning your team to align with enterprise projects and initiatives. You need to not only effectively lead your area of responsibility, but to also emerge as an organizational leader who works together with other executives to help set and deliver on enterprise priorities.

OPERATE LIKE A CEO FROM THE GET-GO

If you want to be successful in making these key career transitions, we believe in adopting a "CEO Mindset." In other words, you must begin to operate like an executive from the get-go. One key element of a CEO mindset is to think of your area of responsibility as a business within a business. Think through your business model (e.g., how you create, deliver, and capture value for the business). This means understanding your value proposition and competitive advantage, core capabilities, suppliers, distribution channels, customers, etc. The other key element of a CEO mindset is to develop the scalable habits, behaviors, and fundamentals that are required to be successful at Level 5—regardless of the level you're currently at. This way, when you make the transitions, you're simply scaling existing behaviors vs. having to develop a completely new way to work. The table on the following page demonstrates this idea using the leadership fundamental "Inspire an Aligned Vision" as an example.

ACT NOW

One more important aspect of developing scalable behaviors and habits is to do so before you need them. In other words, when you're at Level 1, focus on developing the fundamentals required to be successful at Level 2, and so on. Don't wait to get promoted first. Many people are hired or given executive-level promotions because of their intelligence and exceptionally developed executive points of view. This makes sense, because the first criterion is ensuring the group leader has a strong perspective on the right way forward. However, those who haven't learned to manage or lead often stumble in roles with considerable responsibility—because simply knowing the way forward doesn't necessarily translate to organizing and motivating a large group of people to start moving in that direction. This is where executive intuition (which, again, is a function of all four fundamentals) comes in; it is of equal importance to the executive point of view. As outlined previously, it takes time and effort to develop executive intuition, and waiting until you're in senior roles to develop it is not the best recipe for success.

INSPIRE AN ALIGNED VISION

Level	What It Could Look Like
L1 **Individual Contributor**	You seek to understand what your team vision is from your manager.
L2 **Manager**	After understanding the general vision of the team you're part of, you work with your direct reports to define an aligned vision for your direct area of responsibility.
L3 **Director**	After understanding the vision of your function and how it aligns with the broader enterprise vision, you establish a team charter for your direct area of responsibility, present at your monthly all-hands meetings, and hand out charters to each team member.
L4 **Functional Executive**	After understanding the enterprise vision, you work with your leadership team to define and align what that means for your function. You obtain perspectives from your peers and key stakeholders and establish a functional charter that is presented to your function at an annual all-hands meeting. Individual charters are handed out to team members, and large posters are displayed in common areas.
L5 **Enterprise Executive**	You work with the executive team to define a compelling enterprise vision and then regularly communicate it to employees in both large-format all-hands meetings and smaller-format team meetings in a way that inspires and links to the work they're doing. You create organizational charters that are displayed in common areas and regularly link progress to the broader organizational vision.

COMPREHENSIVE EXECUTIVE DEVELOPMENT PLAN

We believe in approaching executive development in the same way you'd approach developing a business plan as the CEO. We believe this is not only the most effective way to ensure your development plan is comprehensive and fully aligned with the CEO Mindset concept, but also that it begins the scalable habit formation we outlined earlier.

To begin, let's revisit the Business Planning Cascade from chapter 2, which is the process we use to set enterprise business plans. We'll outline and simplify the key steps, provide an example of what this could look like in a fictional business, and then demonstrate how the same process can be used for your personal development plans.

BUSINESS PLANNING CASCADE

Step One—Define and align around a destination-winning ambition and long-term performance goals and measures.

Step Two—Define and align the general strategy to achieve the long-term ambitions.

Step Three—Cascade the general strategy into specific strategic initiatives.

Step Four—Build a long-term financial plan that reflects all the decisions and planned outcomes in steps one through three.

Step Five—Cascade long-term performance goals into annual performance goals and measures and specific strategic initiatives into specific annual objectives.[1]

---

1   Sometimes a specific annual objective is the same as a specific strategic initiative and sometimes only a part of a specific strategic initiative to be completed for the year.

Step Six—Cascade specific annual objectives into tactical action plans.
Step Seven—Build an annual financial plan that reflects all the decisions and planned outcomes in steps five through six. This will serve as the primary tool to measure progress against annual ambitions.

BUSINESS PLANNING CASCADE

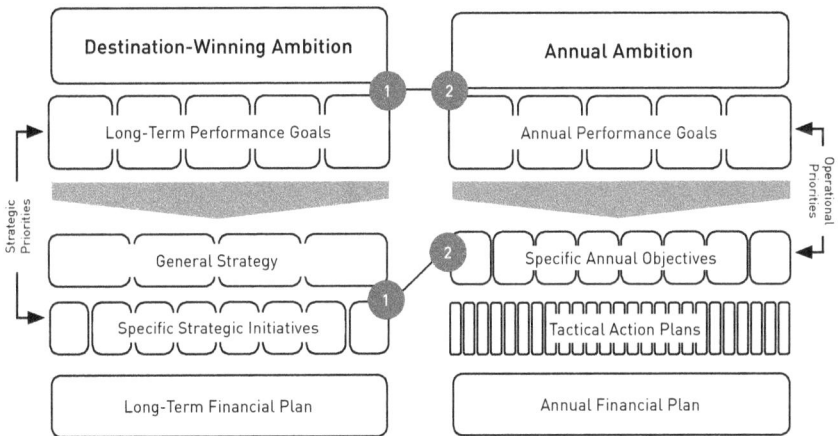

The following figure is an illustration of what this cascade could look like in practice for a fictional business—Asia Pepper Co. Although we've only taken the fictional example as far as the Strategic Priorities, this should help crystallize the cascade process:

Asia Pepper Co. Destination-Winning Ambition

Mission	Vision
We are the intersection of great food that's great for you.	To be the #1 Korean-inspired fast casual destination in the United States.

Long-Term Performance Goals

$1.5B	$150M	85%	95%	60%
10-Yr Revenue	10-Yr Operating Profit	Customer NPS	Employee NPS	Revenue Growth from Product Innovation

General Strategy

Maintain 'recipe-simple, taste-complex' menu that's as nutritious as it is delicious	Deliver best-in-class experience through immaculately kept stores and fast service	Develop efficient, scalable, and replicable operations platform

Strategic Priorities—Specific Strategic Initiatives

National rollout of refreshed menu	Three new store openings in Northeast region	Refresh of Midwest stores	Develop franchise platform	Five store test of new operating model

We can use the same framework to develop your career and executive development plans. Again, this approach serves two purposes: (1) It provides an effective framework to build a development plan, and (2) it catalyzes behaviors and habits that can be scaled throughout career progressions. The chart on the next page titled "Destination-Winning Ambition" outlines what an executive development plan could look like.

From here, continuing to cascade into tactical action plans should be straightforward. For example, the tactical action plan associated with the first strategic initiative, "Align next role with boss that fits experience needs and begin networking with executives in those areas," could look something like this:

January 15	Discuss strengths, development opportunities, and career ambitions with boss.
February 1	Follow-up discussion with boss on potential next role opportunities.
February 15	Document next role opportunities and identify key stakeholders and executives in those areas.
March 30	Schedule and hold one-on-one meetings with stakeholders to build context.
April 15	Refine top three next roles based on stakeholder feedback.
May 1	Schedule initial meetings with key executives in each desired area and request periodic meetings to stay engaged.

Destination-Winning Ambition

Mission

To inspire achievement in others

Vision

To generate profitable growth as an executive leader

Long-Term Performance Goals

4.0	40	10%	20%	65
Years Between Promotions	Age to Achieve Executive Level	Avg. CAGR Base Salary	Annual Income Saved for Retirement	Max Avg. Weekly Hours Worked

General Strategy

Experienced-based Development
Breadth vs. depth with '2x4' role rotations

Develop CEO Mindset
Pursue and lead cross-functional projects to develop fundamentals, institute scalable practices & gain visibility

Knowledge-based Development
Continuous learning through knowledge transfer of others

Specific Strategic Initiatives

- Align next role with boss that fits experience needs and begin networking with executive in those areas

- Lead the development and launch of analyst leadership development program with executive sponsorship

- Develop reading list and process for consolidating notes into development plans

IMPLEMENTING AND MONITORING YOUR DEVELOPMENT PLAN

As we outlined in the Management Ability chapter, planning is only part of the equation. Both doing the work and monitoring execution to course-correct are equally as important. Disaggregating big objectives into individual action items with timelines will give you a road map outlining what you need to do and when. With discipline and the right self-management systems added to the equation, you can hold yourself accountable to actually completing the tasks and course-correcting if certain elements of the plan aren't playing out as expected. It's simple, but it works.

RENTING OR OWNING

With respect to execution, it really all boils down to effort—not only the effort you put forth in developing a career plan, but also the effort you put forth in approaching your role. We believe there are two ways to approach a role. You can "rent" the role or you can "own" the role. This is a useful analogy, because it can be compared to renting vs. owning a home. A great home renter is one who never calls the landlord and who leaves the home in exactly the same condition they found it—earning back the full security deposit. A great homeowner buys the house, repairs all the issues, and remodels with quality material, making the home more livable and valuable than when it was purchased. The same logic can be applied to the roles we hold throughout our career. The question is: Do you want to "rent" and simply occupy a role, or do you want to "own" the role and leave it better than you found it? It's those who own their roles who develop the most and open the doors to new career opportunities.

NO EXCUSES

A reminder: You'll always want to be proactive, so it's important to prevent yourself from falling into the trap of being reactive or a victim of circumstance. Do either of these two excuses sound familiar?

"I'm just doing exactly what my boss asked me to do."

"My boss didn't define any goals or objectives."

In fact, it's better that your boss doesn't define your goals and objectives for you, because it gives you the opportunity to define and align your own. Remember, this doesn't mean you determine your own goals and objectives and then start pursuing them without discussion—aligning is equally as important as defining. Approach every role, regardless of how junior or senior it is, as if you're the CEO of that role with a mindset of ownership, creating value and leaving it better than when you started. This will not only lead to recognition and greater opportunities, but will also develop the unconscious behaviors and habits within yourself that will be the foundation for success in roles with greater responsibility.

ADOPT SELF-MANAGEMENT SYSTEMS

With respect to monitoring execution, we think it's important to adopt self-management systems similar to those we described in the Management Ability chapter. Self-management systems should be customized to fit each individual's work style. They should be thought of as the key daily, weekly, and monthly disciplines needed to monitor not only implementation of your development plan, but also your progress with respect to the responsibilities of your role. Here are a few examples to get started:

DAILY PREP AND PLANNING

At the start of each morning, reviewing your daily schedule and outlining key action items that need to be delivered by the end of the day is a discipline that will ensure you're well prepared.

WEEKLY PREP AND PLANNING

At the end of each week, you should schedule time to prepare and plan for the upcoming week. This is a great opportunity to outline a checklist of all the key action items that need to be delivered and review key meetings that you need to prepare for.

MONTHLY REVIEWS

Similar to a business review, this could be a one-hour monthly review where you're reviewing progress on your development tactical action plans and revising as needed. This should also serve as an opportunity to review progress and performance on the objectives and goals you're being held accountable for in your role.

MEETING PREPARATION

Every meeting is an opportunity to build credibility with those above, below, and diagonal to you. Preparing for meetings in terms of what perspectives you can contribute, what questions you should ask, and a general understanding of your value-add for being there is critical and requires preparation. Lack of preparation can lead to either sitting in silence and not participating or providing perspectives that are off base. Both will damage your credibility.

TRACK PERSONAL WINS AND SETBACKS

To measure and monitor your personal performance and progress, tracking key wins and setbacks is a simple tool. You can start by setting a win-to-setback goal (e.g., 10–1 wins-to-setbacks) and then recording your actual results each week. This serves two key purposes: First, it's a reminder that despite inevitable setbacks, you're delivering considerably more wins. And if you're not achieving your win-to-setback goal, it's a reminder you need to improve. Second, it provides a record of setbacks so that you can learn from them and course-correct.

SELF-ASSESSMENT

The goal of the following self-assessment is to give you an objective view of where you currently sit on the executive fundamentals spectrum and to showcase which areas require development as you hope to make each fundamental a part of your unconscious competence.

We've structured the scoring on a scale of -40 to +40. If your score is in positive territory, it means you've got more developed fundamentals than development opportunities, with the opposite if you're scoring in negative territory. We've chosen this scoring scale because it emphasizes the importance of developing all the fundamentals vs. relying on a few key strengths. Moreover, this assessment is designed to be completed by you, so be as honest and objective as you can.

HERE'S HOW TO SCORE YOURSELF ACROSS EACH FUNDAMENTAL

Score yourself a -2 if you believe you're unconsciously incompetent in any fundamental skill. If you're just becoming aware of a specific skill now, there's a good chance you're in the "not knowing what you don't know" camp.

Score yourself a -1 if you believe you're consciously incompetent in any particular fundamental. This means you're aware of the importance of the fundamental but are uncomfortable with your skill set and haven't yet put any effort into developing it.

Score yourself a +1 if you believe you're consciously competent in any particular fundamental. This is where, when you're focused and concentrating, you feel you've got a satisfactory skill.

Score yourself a +2 if you believe you're unconsciously competent in that particular fundamental. This is where you don't have to think about it, the skill set is ingrained in your subconscious "muscle-memory."

	UI	CI	CC	UC	Score
Business Acumen	-2	-1	1	2	
Strategic Thinking					
Economic Acumen					
Financial Acumen					
Operational Acumen					
Market Orientation					
Management Ability	-2	-1	1	2	
Situational Assessment					
Setting Priorities					
Comprehensive Planning					
Organizing for Action					
Monitoring Implementation					
Leadership Ability	-2	-1	1	2	
Setting the Example					
Inspiring an Aligned Vision					
Empowering Others and Enabling Action					
Challenging the Status Quo					
Encouraging and Motivating					
Executive Intelligence	-2	-1	1	2	
Emotional Awareness					
Emotional Management					
Executive Gravitas					
Executive Communication					
Development Awareness					

KEY

UI	Unconscious Incompetence
CI	Conscious Incompetence
CC	Conscious Competence
UC	Unconscious Competence

CHAPTER 6

BRINGING IT ALL TOGETHER

"Success always demands a greater effort."

—WINSTON CHURCHILL

We believe that executive effectiveness is measured by the quality and consistency of the outcomes you are responsible for delivering. Outcomes are enhanced by better decision-making, which is improved by developing your executive point of view and executive intuition. To do that, you've got to develop your executive fundamentals.

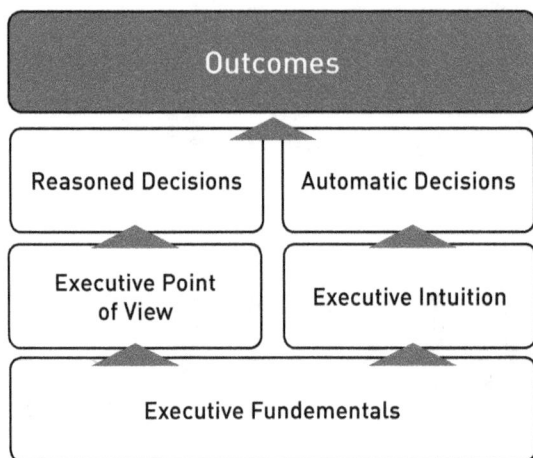

In short, the goal of having well-developed executive fundamentals is to empower groups of people to work together to deliver exceptional results.

To truly become an exemplary executive, we emphasize having well-rounded fundamentals—business acumen, management ability, leadership ability, and executive intelligence—and constantly looking to improve them to ensure they work together to bring out the best in yourself and to help those around you achieve what they never thought was possible.

Executing on the fundamentals can help catalyze a culture where accountability and inclusion are reinforced.

What can be accomplished by bringing together the hearts and minds of the collective is far greater than any individual effort.

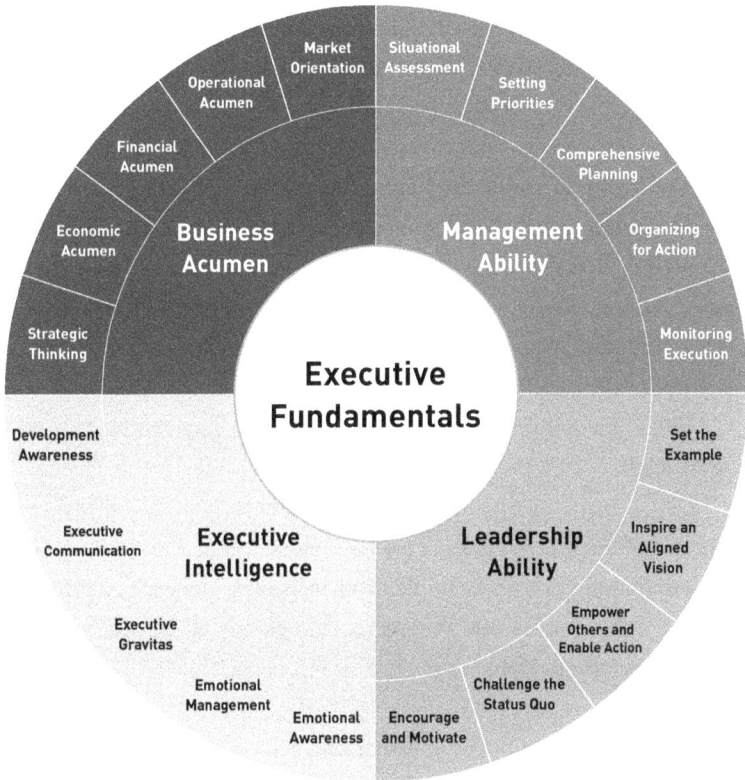

In an interview with Alan Mulally, he was asked about his leadership style, and he responded with this: "Positive leadership—conveying the idea that there is always a way forward—is so important, because that is what you are here for—to figure out how to move the organization forward. Critical to doing that is reinforcing the idea that everyone is included. Everyone is part of the team, and everyone's contribution is respected, so everyone should participate."[1]

---

1   Alan Mulally, "Leading in the 21st century: An interview with Ford's Alan Mulally," interview by Rik Kirkland, *McKinsey & Company*, November 2013, website, https://www.mckinsey.com/business-functions/strategy-and-corporate-finance/our-insights/leading-in-the-21st-century-an-interview-with-fords-alan-mulally.

What can be accomplished by bringing together the hearts and minds of the collective is far greater than any individual effort.

. . .

As you begin to study the habits, behaviors, and conduct of our leaders today—world leaders, business leaders, your own executive team—you'll realize they're simply a representation of their own value systems. And it's no different for us as individuals. Our framework embodies what we believe in and reflects the values we strive to exemplify every day.

Ours is a simple formula: effort, integrity, accountability, and knowledge.

Effort—There is no substitute for hard work and determination. We believe in doing whatever it takes to consistently deliver exceptional results. There is only one thing that trumps raw talent and natural ability, and that's effort.

Integrity—Integrity is the internal character that defines us. It is important that you remain authentic, think about what you believe in, and ensure that your actions accurately reflect those beliefs. We hold the highest ethical and moral standards at all times—both in and out of the spotlight. This is perhaps the most important principle we hold ourselves to—it always demands truth and honesty, which we believe are critical ingredients to challenging, developing, and managing yourself and those around you.

Accountability—We take ownership and never look to make excuses. We own the outcomes of our work, an attitude that is deeply rooted in our DNA. When we fail, we face it head-on, take responsibility, and look for ways to overcome those challenges and succeed the second time around.

Knowledge—Competency is a function of experience and knowledge. We're all born with a certain level of intelligence, which is something we can't change. Knowledge has to be earned.

■ ■ ■

Working hard, holding ourselves accountable, acquiring knowledge, and always doing the right thing has served as a simple set of guardrails guiding our everyday decisions.

Ben Hogan believed that by mastering the four fundamentals of golf, nearly anyone can shoot under 80. For the non-golfers reading this, shooting under 80 is spectacularly difficult. Although there is no "score" to measure executive effectiveness, mobilizing teams and organizations to consistently deliver exceptional outcomes is a close proxy. Similar to mastering golf fundamentals, we believe mastering executive fundamentals requires committing to a journey that takes many years of proactive self-development. It takes discipline to overcome a lack of motivation, focus to generate wins, the ability to learn from setbacks, and an endless drive to improve. Like Hogan's claim for golf, we believe that nearly anyone willing to put forth the effort and commitment to developing the executive fundamentals can evolve into an exemplary executive. Staring at the top of the mountain from the ground is intimidating, but getting to the top starts with a single step.

Anthony, Scott D., Clark G. Gilbert, and Mark W. Johnson. *Dual Transformation: How to Reposition Today's Business While Creating the Future*. Boston: Harvard Business Review Press, 2017.

Azzarello, Patty. *Rise: 3 Practical Steps for Advancing Your Career, Standing Out as a Leader, and Liking Your Life*. New York: Crown Publishing Group, 2010.

Bates, Suzanne. *All the Leader You Can Be: The Science of Achieving Extraordinary Executive Presence*. Texas: McGraw-Hill, 2016.

Baye, Michael. *Managerial Economics & Business Strategy*. Texas: McGraw-Hill, 2005.

Berman, Karen, Joe Knight, and John Case. *Financial Intelligence: A Manager's Guide to Knowing What the Numbers Really Mean*. Boston: Harvard Business School, 2006.

Blenko, Marcia, Eric Garton, and Ludovica Mottura. "Winning Operating Models That Convert Strategy to Results." *Bain & Company* (December 10, 2014). http://www.bain.com/publications/articles/winning-operating-models-that-convert-strategy-to-results.aspx.

Bradberry, Travis, and Jean Greaves. *Emotional Intelligence 2.0*. California: TalentSmart, 2009.

Clawson, James. *Level Three Leadership*. New Jersey: Pearson Education Inc., 2011.

Colley, John, Jr., Jacqueline L. Doyle, Robert D. Hardie, George W. Logan, and Wallace Stettinius. *Principles of General Management*. Connecticut: Yale University Press, 2007.

Collins, Jim. "Level 5 Leadership: The Triumph of Humility and Fierce Resolve." *Harvard Business Review* (July-August 2005). https://hbr.org/2005/07/level-5-leadership-the-triumph-of-humility-and-fierce-resolve.

Cope, Kevin. *Seeing the Big Picture: Business Acumen to Build Your Credibility, Career, and Company*. Texas: Greenleaf Book Group Press, 2012.

Drucker, Peter. *The Practice of Management*. New York: HarperCollins, 1954.

Eblin, Scott. *The Next Level—What Insiders Know About Executive Success*. Boston: Nicholas Brealey, 2011.

Fleisher, Craig, and Babette Bensoussan. *Business and Competitive Analysis: Effective Application of New and Classic Methods*. New Jersey: Pearson Education Inc., 2007.

Goffee, Robert, and Gareth Jones. *Why Should Anyone Be Led by You?: What It Takes to Be an Authentic Leader*. Boston: Harvard Business School. 2015.

Goldsmith, Marshall. *What Got You Here Won't Get You There: How Successful People Become Even More Successful*. New York: Hyperion Books, 2008.

Goleman, Daniel. "What Makes a Leader?" *Harvard Business Review* (January 2004).

Goleman, D., Richard Boyatzis, and Annie McKee. *Primal Leadership: Unleashing the Power of Emotional Intelligence*. Boston: Harvard Business School, 2013.

Heath, Chip, and Dan Heath. *Switch: How to Change Things When Change Is Hard*. New York: Broadway Books, 2010.

Heifetz, Ronald, and Donald Laurie. "The Work of Leadership." *Harvard Business Review* (December 2001). https://hbr.org/2001/12/the-work-of-leadership.

Hewlett, Sylvia Ann. *Executive Presence: The Missing Link Between Merit and Success*. New York: Harper Collins, 2014.

Hoffman, Bryce. *American Icon: Alan Mulally and the Fight to Save Ford Motor Company*. New York: Crown Business, revised 2012.

Hogan, Ben. *Five Lessons: The Modern Fundamentals of Golf*. New York: Simon & Schuster, revised 1985.

Kahneman, Daniel. *Thinking, Fast and Slow*. New York: Farrar, Straus and Giroux, 2013.

Kaplan, Saul. *The Business Model Innovation Factory: How to Stay Relevant When the World is Changing*. New Jersey: John Wiley & Sons, Inc., 2012.

Koller, T., Marc Goedhart, and David Wessels. *Valuation: Measuring and Managing the Value of Companies.* New Jersey: John Wiley & Sons, 2015.

Kotter, John. *Leading Change.* Boston: Harvard Business School, 2012.

Kotter, John. *What Leaders Really Do.* Boston: Harvard Business Review, 1999.

Kouzes, James, and Barry Posner. *The Leadership Challenge.* New Jersey: John Wiley & Sons, Inc., 2017.

Lafley, A.G., and Roger Martin. *Playing to Win: How Strategy Really Works.* Boston: Harvard Business School, 2013.

Levitt, Theodore. *Marketing Myopia.* Boston: Harvard Business School, 2004.

Maital, Shlomo. *Executive Economics: Ten Tools for Business Decision Makers.* New York: Simon & Schuster Inc., 1994.

Maxwell, John. *The 5 Levels of Leadership: Proven Steps to Maximize Your Potential.* New York: Center Street, 2011.

Mulally, Alan. "Working Together: Principles and Practices."

Paris, Joseph F., Jr. *State of Readiness: Operational Excellence as Precursor to Becoming a High-Performance Organization.* Texas: Greenleaf Book Group Press, 2017.

Porter, Michael. *Competitive Strategy: Techniques for Analyzing Industries and Competitors.* New York: The Free Press, 1980.

Shea, Gregory, and Cassie Solomon. *Leading Successful Change: 8 Keys to Making Change Work*. Pennsylvania: Wharton Digital Press, 2013.

Sokol, David L. *Pleased But Not Satisfied*. David Sokol, 2008.

NICK FISCHER is a seasoned executive with broad industry experience spanning consumer packaged goods, banking, retail, and business services. As a complement to his significant corporate finance background, Nick has emerged as both a strategic and operationally oriented leader. With extensive experience at Fortune 500 and middle-market businesses, he has demonstrated consistent success in leading organizational change to drive performance improvement. Nick has focused a significant portion of his career on redefining the traditional role of corporate finance as a true strategic partner at the center of business performance optimization, a topic he regularly addresses through various publications and public speaking engagements.

DAN SHIN is a data-driven executive with a background crossing multiple industries including retail, pharmaceuticals, and business services. He understands the power of information and has dedicated his career to developing analytics-driven organizations that optimize business outcomes. Dan's executive management style and his ability to simplify analytics work flow to deploy actionable insights and recommendations have provided continued success in multiple contexts ranging from start-ups to middle-market and Fortune 500 companies.

www.ingramcontent.com/pod-product-compliance
Lightning Source LLC
Chambersburg PA
CBHW021103210326
41598CB00016B/1313